Lizzie

Lizzie

A VICTORIAN LADY'S AMAZON ADVENTURE

Compiled by

Tony Morrison, Ann Brown & Anne Rose

BRITISH BROADCASTING CORPORATION

Lizzie's sometimes idiosyncratic spelling (dysentry, accordian, inflamation, lillies) has been retained in the letters, but her use of the comma as opposed to other punctuation marks has occasionally been edited in the interests of clarity.

Published by the British Broadcasting Corporation
35 Marylebone High Street, London W1M 4AA

First published 1985

© Tony Morrison, Ann Brown, Anne Rose 1985

ISBN 0 563 20424 9

Typeset in 11 on 13 pt Goudy Roman Linotron by
Ace Filmsetting Ltd, Frome, Somerset

Printed in England by
Butler & Tanner Ltd and St Edmunsbury Press
Colour separations by Wenscan Graphics
Colour printed by Chorley & Pickersgill Ltd

Contents

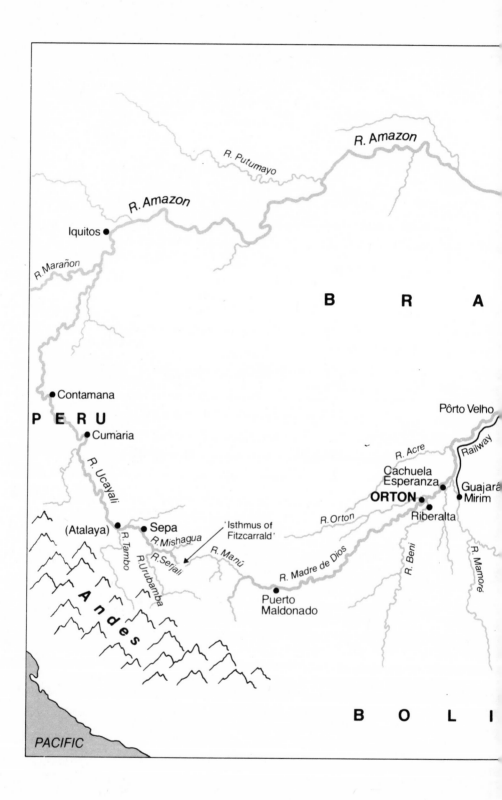

R. Negro

R. Amazon

Manaus

R. Madeira

Z I L

V I A

PANAMA

VENEZUELA

GUIANAS

COLOMBIA

Equator

ECUADOR

Pará
(Belém)

PERU

ORTON

BRAZIL

BOLIVIA

PARAGUAY

CHILE

PACIFIC OCEAN

ATLANTIC OCEAN

URUGUAY

ARGENTINA

Introduction

Lizzie Hessel, the writer of these fascinating letters, lived during the golden age of the British Empire and its influence in world affairs. During her childhood those larger-than-life figures Gladstone and Disraeli were alternate occupiers of 10 Downing Street, and the whole nation mourned when General Gordon, the archetypical Victorian hero, was murdered by the Mahdi's fanatics at Khartoum. In 1887, when Lizzie was a girl, Victoria, the revered Queen-Empress, celebrated her Golden Jubilee; ten years later, while young Mrs Hessel was a thousand miles up the Amazon, anxious for news of home, that pomp and pageantry would be repeated for the Diamond Jubilee. Vast areas of the map were coloured red – nearly one-fifth of the world's surface was a British possession of one kind or another. Although British colonies in South and Central America were few and Spanish and Portuguese interests were paramount, Britain's trading influence, with close links to the City of London, remained strong. It was in a climate of unabashed optimism, therefore, that Lizzie and her husband Fred set out for the rich rubber forests in 1896 with a contract from a London-based company. They were young, adventurous and ambitious: their aim, like that of the *conquistadores* four centuries before them, was simply to get rich.

Had Lizzie not been one of a large, close-knit family her story might never have been written. Those of many other intrepid contemporary travellers who went to raise the flag in some lonely outpost went unrecorded. But Lizzie was determined to maintain contact with her family back home, and anxious to share with them some of the strange sights and experiences of her new life. So she wrote letters – as well as a diary, which was sadly lost in an accident – and, remarkably, most of them have survived. Correspondence between London and Bolivia could take six months to get to its destination; indeed it did not always arrive, for it was subject to all the hazards of primitive methods of transport in inhospitable country. Yet the letters arrived, were read and reread, especially by her younger sister Nell, who treasured this legacy of Lizzie's short but eventful life until her death in 1975.

It is thanks to Lizzie's great-niece, Ann Brown, that these letters are now being published. Ann's parents first showed them to her in the late 1970s; intrigued by what she read on the fading sheets of paper, Ann asked a close friend, Anne Rose, to help her research Lizzie's story more fully. They started with London archives, and then expanded the scope of their exhaustive investigations to other parts of the world. Dr John Hemming of the Royal Geographical Society, knowing of my travels along the Amazon tributaries that are central to Lizzie's own experiences, put Ann Brown in touch with me, and in due course I found myself undertaking the fascinating task of setting Lizzie's letters into context.

The Manú River, where Lizzie spent Christmas 1897, is known today for its rich wildlife and attendant conservation problems, and for the hostility of the forest Indians; it lay on a route which I was following with my wife in 1969, while we were making a film. We spent fifteen days canoeing up the Manú until our guides warned us that it would be dangerous to go further. We were aiming for a passage between two rivers, hidden deep in the rain forest. Bearing in mind, also, that a party of geologists exploring for oil the previous year had been attacked, we decided that discretion was the better part of valour and went back downriver to camp. At that point our guides exercised even greater discretion and left us.

The following morning we found human footprints within ten paces of our shelter. Somewhere – not far away – there were Indians watching us. We believed that the night-time prowlers had been Amahuaca, who have a bad reputation for attacking intruders; later another tribe, the Yaminawa, was suggested: both had suffered at the hands of rubber gatherers and understandably had no love for the white man. We retreated hastily, and back at base my wife was congratulated. Apart from a missionary who had been flown in by light aircraft, the river experts told us, Marion was the first white woman to venture so far upriver. Our surprise, when we first saw Lizzie's letters some years later, was therefore only exceeded by our admiration, for this Victorian lady had over half a century earlier successfully completed the same arduous, dangerous journey on which we had failed.

Some of the letters may seem to gloss over certain things that would alarm or horrify us today. But Lizzie was writing to her family, whom, we can assume, she would not wish to worry with details of disease and squalor; rather, she wanted to talk about things of interest to them, such as the Amazon wildlife and her social life. It is easy for us today to feel and express indignation about injustice, but we should not judge Lizzie from the viewpoint of the late twentieth century. She belonged to a different society, one in which women on the whole accepted the idea of the superior wisdom of husbands and fathers; even though the Suffragette movement was just beginning, there were many thousands of women who outrightly opposed it. Lizzie was conditioned not to enquire, not to pass judgement on matters that were not regarded as part of a woman's sphere of influence.

The only aspect of Lizzie's character as revealed in these letters that does seem strange is her curious lack of real pity towards creatures which many Victorian ladies would have felt were deserving of their affection and protection – children and animals. True, she talks of her pets at great length, but when they die or go missing her grief is minimal, and only lasts until they are replaced. Her comments on her little servant girl eating her dress appear to be made more in a spirit of curiosity than in one of pity. The habitual floggings handed out to the Indians, which initially shocked and revolted her – 'two girls and a boy . . . were chained up and then beaten until they were so exhausted they did not cry any more . . . I was so sick I had to get away from the house,' – later became more acceptable: 'it is the only remedy, of nothing else are they afraid.' She may, of course, merely have been repeating ideas put into her head by Fred or others in the rubber trade. And on the other hand, she seems to have enjoyed friendly relationships with some of the Indian children and to have cared for the Indians when they were stricken with yellow fever.

If there is one thing that Lizzie's tale has brought home to me it is that most of the so-called unexplored places in South America were visited many years ago by travellers such as Lizzie. Courageous and uncomplaining, they would sit, often in appalling conditions, painstakingly writing those letters and diaries which bring to life the bare facts of history:

> The mosquitos are terrible, I had quite 3 dozen in a piece of paper which I murdered whilst writing this letter, but my blackbird has carried them off, otherwise I would have sent them to you. They are splendid in the soup, we eat a lot of them in the season.

Tony Morrison

The Characters in
Lizzie's Story

THE MATHYS FAMILY

Lizzie (Elizabeth) Hessel, née Mathys, born on 21 April 1870, was one of the ten children of *John Mathys* and *Sarah Jane Treble*. Lizzie's sisters were *Alice*, *Frances* (nicknamed *Rose* or *Rosie*), *Edith* (*Bib*), *Louisa* (*Lou*) and *Helen* (*Nell*). Her brothers were *John* (*Jack*), *Frederick*, *George* and *Albert* (*Bert*).

THE HESSEL FAMILY

Fred (Frederick) Joseph Hessel, born in 1863, was one of the eleven children of *Johannes Augustus Hessel* and *Eva Wisger*. His nephew *Frederick A. Hessel* was born in 1898 and in 1985 was still alive in the USA. Other members of the family are settled in Antwerp, Malta and Bordeaux.

Arana, Julio César

A Peruvian rubber trader and businessman born in Yurimaguas, at the foot of the Andes, he eventually created a million-pound company based in London.

Casement, Roger David

Born in Kingstown (now Dun Laoghaire) in Co. Dublin, he became known for his investigation of cruelty to local labour in the Belgian Congo. He was British Consul-General in Rio de Janeiro and was asked to investigate a scandal involving atrocities and a British company in the Putumayo region of Peru and Colombia. Later he travelled to New York to seek aid for the Irish Easter Rising against the British. He was subsequently hanged for treason in 1916.

Fawcett, Percy Harrison

Born in Torquay in 1867, he joined the Royal Artillery. As a surveyor, he was seconded to a commission establishing some of the boundaries of Bolivia, Peru and Brazil in unexplored Amazon forests. He disappeared, it is believed, in the Mato Grosso of Brazil in 1925.

Fitzcarrald, Carlos Fermín

Born in 1862, he was one of seven sons of a US sailor who settled in Peru. He became known as the Rubber Spy from his suspected contact with hostile Chile when he was a student. He explored and developed the waterway and land route in the heart of the Peruvian rubber forests which is still known as the Isthmus of Fitzcarrald. The German film director *Werner Herzog* made a personal interpretation of his life in the film *Fitzcarraldo*.

Hardenburg, Walter Ernest

A North American railway engineer and scholar who was outraged by the inhumane treatment of Amazon Indians on the Putumayo River, he carried the story to London, undaunted by threats to his life.

Heath, Edwin
A US doctor and explorer, after working with a company involved with the Madeira–Mamoré railway he completed the exploration of the Beni River in Bolivia. He was a friend of *Antonio Vaca Diez*.

Orton, James
A US naturalist and explorer from Philadelphia, he taught natural history at Vassar College. He made three expeditions to South America, including an attempted exploration of the Beni which was brought to a halt when his Indian partners deserted.

Suárez, Don Francisco
The eldest of the Suárez brothers was Bolivian Consul-General in London. He ran the family business affairs from offices in the City.

Suárez, Don Nicholás
One of six sons and two daughters; his two youngest brothers, *Oscar* and *Antonio*, died young. With his brothers *Francisco*, *Gregorio* and *Romuló* he developed Bolivian rubber, ranching and transport enterprises. Their 'empire', based in Bolivia and London, extended to property in Hampstead.

Suárez, Don Pedro
Son of *Gregorio Suárez*, he married *Jessie*, *Cecil Beaton*'s aunt. He became Military Attaché at the Bolivian Legation in London and later Consul-General.

Vaca Diez, Dr Antonio
A doctor, explorer and scholar with political and business acumen, he founded a newspaper, *La Gaceta del Norte*, and the Orton (Bolivia) Rubber Co. Ltd. He was married to *Sra Lastenia Franco*, and they had six children including a son, *José Oswaldo*.

Wickham, Henry Alexander
He travelled in the tropical Americas, finally settling in Santarém on the Amazon, and collected rubber seeds which he despatched to the Royal Botanic Gardens at Kew.

Chapter One

'You can have everything you wish for except money'

On a damp August Saturday in London in 1892 two young people from respectable though modest backgrounds, Lizzie Mathys and Fred Hessel, were married. The relatives and friends gathered at St Saviour's Church in Hampstead would have considered them no different from any other late Victorian couple about to start on a new life together, with the responsibilities of running a home and providing for the large family that, in keeping with the times, they would no doubt produce. But the reality was rather different, for Fred had set his heart on making a fortune in the expanding South American rubber trade, and far from becoming a sober suburban housewife and mother, Lizzie was to accompany him on this romantic and dangerous adventure into wild and frequently uncharted territory.

Fred Hessel, or Fritz as he was known to his family, was a trader with his background firmly secured by a family business. His parents were German, from the city of Mainz on the Rhine. After they married in 1859 Mr Hessel set up offices in London and Bordeaux, and he and his wife divided their time between the two cities. Their first two children, Graham and Maria, were born in London, while Frederick, the third, was born in Bordeaux. The Hessel stock-in-trades were oils, spirit, pitch oil and essence of petrol. As a young man Fred left France to join his Uncle Joseph at the London end of the business, and at the time of his marriage he was working as a commercial clerk at the company's Old Broad Street office in the City.

His bride was twenty-two, slim, effervescent and with an undisguised *joie de vivre*. An outsider might have said she was too active for her own good, but the Mathys' home was always bustling. A 'gregarious place', her sister once called the yellow brick Victorian cottage in De Beauvoir Road, Hackney, then an attractive, thriving middle-class suburb, popular among the families of City workers.

John Mathys, Lizzie's father, was a Swiss cabinetmaker from Rutschelen, a canton of Berne, while her mother, Sarah, had been born in Devon. The couple raised ten children – Lizzie was the third eldest girl after Alice and Rose. From the two parents' widely different origins emerged a succession of visitors who were made welcome in a house already bursting at the seams. Through her parents' example Lizzie learnt to be sociable and adaptable. Life in the Mathys household could not have been happier, even though the children were cramped three or four to a bedroom.

Of her five sisters and four brothers, Lizzie was particularly fond of Bert, seven years younger, whose active mind she admired. Nell, the youngest, was just eight when Lizzie married; she grew up closer to their mother than did any of the other children, and she never married. Before her death in 1975, Nell recollected the days at 83 De Beauvoir Road when Lizzie and Fred were courting. As Nell said: 'Everyone spoke very highly of him, despite what happened.' To her, Fred was just another 'gentleman from overseas' who now and then called on John Mathys to make fine boxes of polished wood for his business. At the time Fred was living on Haverstock Hill, less than three miles away.

Both Fred and Lizzie, coming as they did from entrepreneurial immigrant stock, were ambitious, and not long after their marriage they decided to visit Fred's family and friends in Bordeaux. Nell remembered sitting in the small, leafy garden in Hackney while Lizzie told them wonderful stories of that summer in France, flicking through postcards and family snapshots. Her sister had met a Mrs Haendel, a German woman who spoke English and made her feel at home. For Fred, though, going home to Bordeaux was a routine business trip: it offered him the opportunity to show off his young wife, expenses paid, as well as time to see old friends and to muse about the business project he was dreaming of in the Amazon Basin. Local talk was favourable, as connections were strengthening between Bordeaux and the expanding city of Pará in Brazil, at the mouth of the great river.

Fred knew Pará as the base for Amazon traders: 'Buy for five what is worth twenty and sell for twenty what is worth five' was a well-justified local saying. As regional capital, Pará had become the mecca for an élite who prospered on the rapid upsurge of rubber, most of the world's supply at this time coming from that area. Itinerant merchants moved out from Pará along the Amazon's immense network of waterways, selling everything from manioc flour to kerosene, one of the products dealt in by the Hessels. Fred, it seems, already had experience of the Amazon. According to his nephew, who in 1985 was still alive, at the age of eighty-seven, in the USA: 'Fred was my favourite uncle – as you know, he made several trips to South America on behalf of a British rubber syndicate. At one time, he was wrecked in the Amazon and lived for weeks on bananas.' In her letter of 6 December 1898 Lizzie refers to the birth of this nephew.

But while the Amazon had plenty of rubber, it was low on people. Labour was already in demand by plantation owners for sugar cane working and brazil nut collecting. Then with the development of the rubber trade even more hands were needed, so Pará businesses looked to Mediterranean Europe for workers likely to be best suited to the tropical climate of the Amazon. Bordeaux was a convenient port with a long-established history of trade – in particular the triangular trade, which involved sending arms and wine from France to Africa, then taking slaves from Africa to the West Indies, and finally bringing home from the Caribbean profitable coffee.

Fred could see the opportunities for a businessman with Bordeaux connections, and his heart lay firmly in South America. But he had also experienced the unpredictability of that continent's politics and he was accordingly cautious. They decided to take the matter no further for the present, and returned to London. Fred, however, remained determined as ever to return to South America, and when the right opportunity presented itself a little later this time he did not refuse.

Even in the three years of Lizzie and Fred's marriage the international prospects for rubber had continued to improve. When first discovered, rubber had been thought something of a curiosity: it got its English name from its use as an eraser, and its French name, *caoutchouc*, from a local word, *cahuchu*, meaning 'weeping tree' – rubber started life as a milky latex tapped from certain trees by slashing the bark. But in its raw state not much could be done with rubber, and outside the tropics it melted in summer and went rock-hard in winter. All that changed when in 1839 an American called Charles Goodyear invented vulcanisation, a process in which rubber and sulphur are heated together to yield a substance which remains tough and pliable. Now all kinds of uses, many of them previously only served by leather, were open for rubber: shoes, braces, belting, waterproofing, tyres and even cushions for billiard tables.

The rubber industry took another giant step when, only two years before Lizzie and Fred married, a Scottish veterinary surgeon called John Boyd Dunlop patented the pneumatic tyre for bicycles, which had previously run on slow, spine-jarring solid metal wheels. Cycling now began to boom as both a sport and a pastime. The British public were barraged with persuasive advertisements, frequently depicting winsome young bicycling women, from rival manufacturers: 'Rudge Whitworth Cycles – Smartest and Best', and 'The Bamboo Cycle – for Strength and Rigidity'. Lizzie too was drawn into the craze, riding the bumpy streets of Hackney most respectably in a long dress with a hat tied by a silk scarf under her chin – not for her the more practical but notorious garments named after their originator, Miss Amelia Bloomer.

The horseless carriage, too, was continuing to make news. In the United States a three-wheel, one-cylinder Duryea, though little more than a motorised tricycle, was pop-popping its way to success. Henry Ford was already working in Detroit, and in Europe Karl Benz had produced a four-wheeler as far back as 1885. The world was moving forward on rubber.

In statistical terms, in 1831, before the invention of vulcanisation, the Amazon exported only 31 tons of rubber. By 1880 that figure had risen to over 8000 tons, which doubled to over 16,000 by 1890 and was heading for well over 27,000 tons in 1900.

To supply the rapid growth of the industry in Europe and America, powerful enterprises were emerging in the Amazon. Money, daring and business acumen became the basis for immense personal fortunes wrought from places hardly known about in Europe. Bolivia was one such place, and two Bolivian cousins were to enter the lives of Fred and Lizzie. Then forty-five, moustached, tireless and a master businessman, Nicholás Suárez was one of four brothers. Dr Antonio Vaca Diez was a young politician with a dominating personality, best known for his grandiose plans and arrogant greed for power. Between them these two men controlled a slice of the Amazon Basin half the size of France, though small in South American terms. That region was the Beni or land along the Beni River, whose source lies in the Andes. Vaca Diez also put his mark even further away along the Orton River, a tributary of the Beni, where he had access to rich rubber forests in the no man's land of Acre, on the Bolivian–Brazilian border.

In this far western end of the Amazon, travel upriver is eventually blocked by rapids and forested Andean canyons. In the 1890s any journey to the Bolivian capital, La Paz, set 11,500 feet up in the mountains, meant weeks and often months of nightmarish travel. The hazards of savage Indians, snakes, disease and natural disasters created such a barrier between the mountains and the Amazon lowlands that Suárez and Vaca Diez found it quicker to travel across the Atlantic to Europe than to visit La Paz. Anyway, there was never much love lost between the mountain people of Bolivia and those in the Amazon Beni.

Both men had property in London. The first Suárez to head for that city was Nicholás' eldest brother, Francisco, who had left Bolivia in 1871 at the age of thirty-eight. Francisco settled in Britain, becoming Bolivian Consul-General and opening a City office at 12 Fenchurch Street, first with his own trading company and then in partnership with

Nicholás. Later, when by combining financial and diplomatic interests the Suárez brothers were on their way to becoming millionaires, Francisco set up the European headquarters of Suárez Hermanos & Co.

Nicholás' nephew, Pedro, was educated at Uxbridge School and married Jessie, an aunt of the society photographer Sir Cecil Beaton. In later life Beaton remembered his 'Uncle Percy' and the elegant life at 74 Compayne Gardens, Hampstead, where some of Percy's numerous amorous tangles began, including one with the housemaid, who became pregnant – such a contrast to his uncle Don Nicholás, whose first and greatest love was a lady called Constanza, who died soon after his first successes along the Beni. Nicholás built a marble memorial to her, which still stands beside the river.

Officially, though, London had no interest in Bolivia, a country twice the size of France and in a state of political turmoil. The Bolivians still joke about a story concerning a lively reception said to have been held in 1880 by the President, Narciso Campero. After many insults had been thrown about, Campero raised the flounces of his favourite mistress's skirt and, turning to the British Minister, invited him to kiss her bottom. One version of this apocryphal tale has it that after the Minister politely refused he was run out of La Paz seated backwards on a donkey, jeered abusively by the locals. Appalled by this insult by a petty upstart foreigner to Her Britannic Majesty's august representative, Queen Victoria is said to have ordered a gunboat to stand off the Bolivian coast. On being informed that Bolivia had no coastline, the Queen instructed that Bolivia should be struck off the map of South America, saying that henceforth it would be marked as 'unexplored territory inhabited by savages'.

Not surprisingly, perhaps, the British Foreign Office refused to appoint a professional British diplomat to Bolivia, even less a Vice-Consul in the rubber boom area of the Beni. The official attitude simply could not come to terms with backwoods politics. 'Government? What is that? We know no government here,' commented one rubber tapper to a British traveller.

Scruples, though, never seem to concern certain sectors of the business world, and when Vaca Diez visited London in 1896 he had no trouble in raising capital of £340,500 for a company which he was forming, called the Orton (Bolivia) Rubber Co. Ltd. Among the directors were Francisco Suárez and two Frenchmen living in Paris – Baron Jacques de Gunzburg and Alexandre Devès.

Less flamboyant and with an eye to steady business, the Hessels were buying and selling with Teutonic diligence from an office close to the

Suárez premises. Fred did not have to look far to find his Amazon ambitions rekindled, and he soon realised that he, Vaca Diez and Francisco Suárez had a mutual interest.

Vaca Diez needed a manager for his base or *barraca* at Orton, and Fred seemed to be the man for the job. Someone like Fred, Vaca Diez believed, an accomplished accountant with experience in the Amazon, could keep a firm control on costs, a craft mastered by cousin Nicholás. Also he needed someone young and determined to help him head off any possible takeover threat from the Suárez brothers. Bolivians like Nicholás Suárez and Vaca Diez never considered half-measures, even among themselves. Both found finance in London and Paris and both set their hearts on the rich prize of the best rubber in the Amazon.

As far as Fred was concerned, the position offered by Vaca Diez could not have been better. Lizzie was permitted, possibly even encouraged, to go with him – though men engaged on colonial and similar enterprises were frequently not allowed to take their families with them, and if single were forbidden to marry. There was a house, a secure salary and contract, and all expenses would be paid. Fred now decided to become a naturalised British citizen, for to be British was highly regarded in South America, even in the Beni, and especially in commerce. The fact that even the nearest point on the Orton River was 1500 miles from the Amazon mouth, beyond treacherous rapids bounded by forests concealing wild animals and savages, did not deter Fred and Lizzie.

Their families, too, accepted the challenge, and John and Sarah Mathys took care of the couple's possessions. November and December 1896 were filled with buying all their requirements for a tropical climate, packing, and dealing with a stream of visitors and well-wishers. Exotic placenames such as Bolivia, the Amazon and the Andes were heard so frequently that they became household words. Lizzie was enjoying herself. Adventures lay ahead, though she had no idea of their magnitude, and when interviewed by 'Marie', a columnist for the *Morning Leader*, she uttered phrases that have the ring of a Vaca Diez or Suárez prospectus. The article began:

AN ADVENTUROUS ENGLISHWOMAN WHO
WILL HELP OPEN UP AN UNKNOWN LAND
Where is Bolivia? I had to ask the question, for even I cannot be expected to know the exact location of every place on the surface of the earth.

Lizzie was not the traveller 'Marie' anticipated.

I pictured the lady as tall and muscular with a masculine head, thick short hair combed back from a high forehead, perhaps spectacles –

*anyway large shoes and short skirts. Surely, I thought, when I saw her in
her charming drawing room, this tall, slight girl still under five and
twenty, could not brave the dangers of unexplored lands.*

Lizzie was in fact in her twenty-seventh year, but she had no intention
of being anything other than a lady, attractive and, by her sheer
magnetism, the centre of attention. 'Marie' was shown the clothes,
which had to last five years. Some of the ladies' column's readers must
have envied Lizzie's style, but Lizzie herself may later have regretted
buying so many beautiful things after the Spanish Customs had fingered
each one.

*I went with her and saw an enormous array of cool, pretty muslins,
cotton and zephyr dresses, one after another, spotted, flowered, striped,
in white and all the coolest of pale tints; dressing and teagowns, and
sunshades in dozens. White shoes, stockings and gloves, sailor straws,
leghorn and Panama hats without end. The petticoats and underclothing
were beautiful, of the finest nainsook, Indian muslin and web-like silk.*

Such was Lizzie's idea of life on the Amazon. Money came from trees.
Fred had sensed it and Lizzie intended to savour it. And the dangers?
Lizzie told 'Marie' about the projected journey up the Amazon, where at
one place on a tributary they would face rapids.

*. . . we come to the worst parts, for we have 25 days journey over
cataracts of extreme danger. One in particular has been given the title of
'Cataract do Inferno'.*

'Hell' was left untranslated in Portuguese, perhaps to avoid offending
the lady readers at their breakfast tables. As 'Marie' said to Lizzie:

*'And you will be cut off from the world for five long years. And you
will eat your breakfast with no* Morning Leader *beside your plate.'*

Somehow all the packing was completed, the final emotional good-
byes said. By 15 December they were ready; on the same day Fred's
naturalisation papers were confirmed. Polly, Lizzie's parrot, a gift from
Fred from earlier travels, was entrusted to Carrie – Caroline Straker,
who later married Lizzie's brother George. But Lizzie could not bear to
leave behind Bill Sikes, or Sambo, as her dog was called by the family.
A cab, a four-wheel 'growler', was called, and Fred and the family
loaded the hand baggage on to the roof rack; the larger boxes had
already been sent ahead to the station. The horse's hooves clattered on
the cobbles as they turned to wave their last to family and friends whom
they did not expect to see again for five years.

Their first destination was Paris, where Fred had to see one of the
French directors of the Orton Company. Their journey began prosai-
cally at Holborn Viaduct Station, the London terminus of the London,

Chatham and Dover Railway. As the train rattled above the crush of horse-drawn traffic on Ludgate Hill, Lizzie snatched a final look at the familiar landmark of St Paul's Cathedral. After they had crossed the Thames and ridden high on viaducts over the slate-roofed landscape of suburbia, the view from the train window began to change and they sped through the orchards and hopfields of the Kent countryside until they reached the coast – or the seaside, as Lizzie called it, remembering childhood family outings. At Dover they boarded a 'paddler', probably the *Calais* which was exclusive to the night services of the London, Chatham and Dover Railway; here Lizzie proved to be not the best of sailors, and 'fed the fishes', as she delicately wrote. Next morning they were in Calais, from where the train took them to Paris.

Lizzie's first letter home was from the Grand Hotel in the Boulevard des Capucines.

> Grand Hotel, Boulevard des Capucines 17, Paris
> 16 December 1896
>
> My dear Dad and Ma,
>
> You will see by the above address that we have arrived safely in Paris. We started from Holborn at 9 o'clock and reached Dover at 12 o'clock. We then took the boat and had a lovely moonlight trip, but all the same I fed the fishes. At Calais we took the Paris train and arrived at the large and dirty station at ½ past 6. We then drove here and went to bed. Fred got up at 10 o'clock and went about his business.

For their first night away they could not have done better. Baron Jacques de Gunzburg, who maintained a stylish home in the same boulevard, had booked them into the largest and most elegant hotel in Paris, with 800 rooms, mirrored halls, fluted columns, elegant balconies and ornate wrought ironwork. Sarah Bernhardt had been there just a week before them, and every evening there was music before dinner. Lizzie loved it, and in case she was feeling homesick the exquisite French hospitality even offered afternoon tea.

Typical of the times, Fred kept his wife well separated from his business affairs, and just as typically there was never a hint of resentment from Lizzie that she knew nothing of what he did. She seemed happiest with her own thoughts and the very special position in which she now found herself. Her letter home continues:

> I took it easier and have only just got down at ½ past 1 to the reading room to write to you. We shall not leave Paris until tomorrow, as our business will take longer than we thought, so I shall be able to see a bit of this wonderful city.

This is a most beautiful hotel, the largest in Paris. You have only to ring the electric bell and you can have everything you wish for except money, which disappears very quickly in travelling. The electric light also you switch on and off as you please.

I don't think I have any more news just now, as I have not begun sight seeing yet, but I shall write to you every chance I get. Now goodbye my dear Dad and Mum, with love from Fred and myself to everybody,

From

Your loving daughter

Lizzie

With a day to spare, Lizzie sent a postcard – a reflection on the excellent postal services of the day.

Paris
17 December 1896

Dear Dad and Ma,

Just a few lines to let you know we are still in Paris, we leave tonight at ½ past 10 for Bordeaux. If you write to the following address tomorrow the letter will reach us in Lisbon: c/o Senor Don Luiz A. Collares, Rua do S. Mamede 89, Lisbon.

Yours affectionately

Lizzie

They left from the Gare d'Austerlitz, and on arrival in Bordeaux Lizzie reported:

Bordeaux
18 December 1896

My dear Dad and Mum,

We have reached the next stage of our journey quite safely. We left Paris by the ½ past 10 train, travelled all night, slept in the train and arrived here at 8 o'clock this morning. It was a very tiring journey. Being dark we could not see anything of the country.

Bordeaux offered a break from travelling, and a chance once more to meet the Hessel family and Lizzie's German friend from her previous visit, Mrs Haendel. Lizzie and Fred found time to walk and look at the shops, which she greatly admired, and in the evenings they went to the first French theatre she had ever seen. For Fred there was work to be done, looking after the affairs of Vaca Diez who had just left Bordeaux for Pará with 500 Spanish emigrants.

Madrid was next on the young couple's whistle-stop tour. Lizzie was settling into her new life with obvious pleasure, travelling in sleeping cars with a 'splendid restaurant and well served meals'.

> . . . the scenery from Bayonne to Madrid being splendid, moun-
> tains on either side of us and everywhere covered in snow; about
> every half an hour we passed picturesque little villages, just a
> cluster of houses with a church in the middle. The people travel
> from one to the other on mules and donkeys with the panniers
> either side of them, and look just like brigands, with their bright
> colours and cloaks and slouch hats. They are very nasty looking
> people.

Soon she discovered that travelling with her own exotic wardrobe could
be a problem.

> The Spanish Customs people are very particular. They made us
> pay duty on all my new dresses – took each one out and weighed it
> and bundled it back again anyhow. The silk caught their eye, that
> was something for them. They are all crumpled and do not look
> like new now. Perhaps it is a good thing, for the Portuguese are
> even worse. Fred had to pay £2 duty.

These were Lizzie's first thoughts from Lisbon, where they stayed near
the station at the Avenida Palace Hotel, which had been recommended
to them for its comfort.

It was in Lisbon that Lizzie recorded the first of many frustrations that
were to dog their travels: a continuing dock strike in Hamburg delayed
the arrival of the steamer taking them to Brazil. In London, before they
left, *The Times* had reported cautiously on the 'probability of an even-
tual victory of the employers', saying on 14 December that 200 strikers
had 'resumed work on the old terms'. The *Illustrated London News*
speculated that the English had engineered the strike 'to upset the
manufacturing and trading community'. But Lizzie was not concerned
with the political background, for the delay gave her more time in
Lisbon to go sightseeing and to enjoy some unusually mild weather for
the time of year:

> You cannot imagine, so white and sunny, it is like a summer's
> day. I had to put up my umbrella for the sun. We shall have to stay
> here for 5 days, we think, as our steamer is delayed at Hamburg on
> account of the strikes, so we shall have a chance of seeing Lisbon.
> The living here is good too, and all accommodation is good.

In the same letter, which boasted a rare P S from the hard-working Fred,
Lizzie mentions the name of the steamer, the *Sobralense* of the Red
Cross Line, which was to take them on the next stage of their journey:

> I was glad to get your letter this morning. Your next one must be
> addressed to *Sobralense* Madeira.
>
> I hope you will all have a jolly Xmas and a happy New Year, and

think of us when you are having your dinner. I do not know where we shall be until our steamer arrives.

With love to all and to yourselves, especially, from your loving daughter,

Lizzie

Kind regards to all, Fred.

On Christmas Eve 1896 Lizzie and Fred were still in Lisbon. Her next letter gives the impression that, while frustrated, she is still making the most of the extra time. Her descriptive details of Lisbon rise above the first touches of homesickness – although it was the time of year when the rest of the family would all be together.

Avenida Palace, Lisbon

24 December 1896

My dear Dad and Ma,

Our steamer has not arrived at Oporto yet so we do not expect to start again until Sunday or Monday. I am impatient to be on the way again and wish she would hurry up. I am enclosing a small view of the sleeping car in which we travelled and also a piece of my dessert from last night's dinner – it is off one of the small oranges which grow here. They are very nice and sweet.

Please tell all the boys and girls that they must start writing to Orton soon. We shall want news from home badly after our long journey. I shall expect them all to write, every one of them.

We went for a lovely walk this afternoon, high up in the town from where we got a splendid view of Lisbon; it is a very large town.

There does not seem much preparation for Xmas going on here, except for the turkeys which they take through the streets 20 or 30 of them together. They drive them with long sticks, fine birds they are too and quite tame; he whistles to them and they come running along.

I suppose Rose and Ben are settled with you now for Xmas. I am looking forward to news of you all again, which I expect we shall get at Madeira.

Rose was Lizzie's sister Frances, whom John Mathys had once likened to a rose, after which the nickname had stuck. At sixteen Rose married Ben Edwards, who somehow maintained a precarious business trading in photographic chemicals; Lizzie was always concerned for their future. She continued:

The trams here rush about at such a rate you feel sure you will be turned over sometime or other: if there is a cart or anything in front of them, they simply get off the lines and pass them. Sometimes they don't use the lines at all; if it is very hilly they have 5 mules on one tram. They are queer people here.

Now I have no more news, so with love to you and everybody from your loving daughter,

Lizzie

The steamer arrived in Lisbon on Christmas Day. At last their bundles and boxes were carefully stowed aboard. The small *Sobralense*, only 1982 tons gross but stately and well appointed, was owned by the Liverpool firm of R. Singlehurst and Co. which had been working the route to northern Brazil fortnightly for many years. Out to Madeira Lizzie kept to her bunk, though she was well enough to make the acquaintance of the four other passengers.

They spent just one day in Madeira and braved going ashore in small boats, breaking through the surf by waiting for an Atlantic roller to carry them in. For Lizzie it was a relief to have her feet on firm ground for a few hours. She was amused by the way the 'native boys came along in boats asking for us to throw coins into the water, for which they dived right under the ship to the other side – but they must be silver coins,' she added, 'for copper they will not go in.' It was Fred who had to send the customary note home; he had made the crossing before, and found his sea legs quickly.

SS *Sobralense*, Madeira Island
29 December 1896

Dear Dad and Dear Ma,

I write for Lizzie this time, as she feels still a bit sickly. We have had very fine weather between Lisbon and here, but Lizzie is and always will be a very bad sailor. She is, however, recovering quickly now and the rest of the journey is bound to be very smooth. It always is.

We shall arrive in Pará in about 10 days time and will, then, of course, write you again.

With love to all,
Yours affectionately
Fred

Chapter Two

'The best part of the journey is to come'

'The entrance to the Amazon is very disappointing,' wrote Lizzie. 'It is very thick and sandy water, though I have never seen such lovely skies.' She had been ill as usual during the long crossing, so her disenchantment is understandable.

Coming in from the Atlantic, it is hard to tell where sea ends and the river begins. A fifth of the world's fresh water is locked into the Amazon system, and every second seven and a half million cubic feet of water pour from its mouth; 150 miles off the coast the water is still fresh, so when the Spanish navigator Yáñez Pinzón and his men discovered the river in 1500 they called it Santa María de la Mar Dulce, soon shortened to La Mar Dulce or Sweetwater Sea.

Lizzie had little idea of the scale of the Amazon when she said, 'Of course the best part of the journey is to come – I am very glad it is river and not sea.' She was at the mouth of the greatest river in the world: it stretches right across the widest part of South America to a source within 60 miles of the Pacific Ocean on the other side of the continent. Fifty thousand miles of waterways lay ahead of Lizzie, spreading out like the veins and arteries of a giant body. By 1897 the main network was known, and nerve centres governing the region's activity had been established.

Pará, now Belém, stands 90 miles upriver, and more precisely on the Pará River which empties some of the Amazon on the southern side. Boats of all kinds trading between islands fill the harbour. A market at the water's edge begins at dawn as local farmers and fishermen arrive, many of whom have been travelling for days by sailing boat. By 1897 Pará was already a prosperous city and its port the centre of rubber trade activity for the entire river. Warehouses, shipping offices, import–export offices, bars and sleazy places of assignation lined the waterfront. Many of the buildings were occupied by *aviadores*, the traders who dealt with rubber holdings upriver. People of various nationalities, both South American and European, crowded the streets.

Fred and Lizzie breakfasted on the *Sobralense* and went ashore at 10 a.m., taking their trunks and boxes directly to the modest and decaying Hotel Central. The day was already hot and Lizzie, unaccustomed to the humidity, said that she 'perspired dreadfully'. But Fred, a steely character who had been through it all before, was soon back at work. 'Fred is A1,' Lizzie remarked, 'he sends his love. He is out on business at present.' Pará thrived on business. Vaca Diez had arrived ahead of the *Sobralense*, and immediately he and Fred began planning the long journey to Orton. The 500 Spanish immigrants which Vaca Diez had brought from Bordeaux were causing problems.

Amazon politics in the 1890s, particularly those in Pará, were closely linked with the land around the city, and to the east in particular the forest was being cleared for crops. Labour was the base of every enterprise, not because the cost was high but because the supply was desperately short. Tapping trees for rubber took people from the land, and as money could be made from both land and rubber the argument for priorities swayed back and forth. Immigration was encouraged and financial incentives were established by law No. 233, passed in Pará on 20 June 1894.

Among other measures the authorities of the state of Pará decided to hire two firms to recruit, transport and look after the resettling of 35,000 immigrants. The state agreed to subsidise the cost of shipping people across the Atlantic and to provide temporary accommodation in Pará on arrival. Clearly, a lot of money was to be made. One sum of about 15,000 dollars was paid by the state for land on which to build an immigrant 'hotel' – this was a disproportionately large payment, but then the land in question belonged to Innocencia Baena, the Secretary of State's brother.

Every *aviador* or supplier, exchange dealer or lady of pleasure at any point on the social scale was making money. It was all too easy. Being friendly with the director of a local bank helped, and a business deal could be started with little or no capital. An entrepreneur would begin by registering his firm with a capital of perhaps 1000 dollars, which of course he did not have either as cash or as security. The friendly banker, persuaded by favours, would release money which would then be used for buying shares in his bank; these shares could be used at another bank as collateral against which a certain amount of cash could be borrowed. Then, with money once again in hand, the dealer could deposit it in a third bank. A lot of legwork was involved and an excess of black *cafezinhos* – small coffees 'as black as night, as sweet as a kiss, as strong as love and hot as hell', as they are commonly described in South America – were sipped on the way to respectability. The trader was now suddenly both a stockholder and a depositor, and he had two banks willing to give him a reference. Thereafter the credit rating of his firm depended entirely on his skill as an operator.

Vaca Diez, however, with £340,000 behind him in London, was in Pará to try his luck with bigger risks. Lizzie, obviously knowing only part of the story, talked about him in one of her letters home.

Hotel Central, Pará

18 January 1897

My dear Dad and Ma,

We are still in Pará and are likely to stay here for another week. They have such trouble in getting the goods etc. through the Customs, it has taken them 6 weeks already, and during that time Mr Vaca Diez has had to keep all the emigrants and people. By the time we arrive in Orton, he will have lost £60,000. Isn't it dreadful?

In 1896, 3123 Spanish immigrants entered Pará; Vaca Diez, according to Lizzie, brought in 500 of them. How many ships were used is not known, but in those days most vessels were small, so conditions would have been unbearably cramped. But few people cared, and as long as the money flowed smoothly it meant business as usual in Pará.

He has sorted out the emigrants and out of 400 only 100 are coming with us. The others were vagabonds and no good at all. There are about 60 women and children amongst them. They had a most rough and uncomfortable journey from Bordeaux and we are so thankful that we did not travel with them.

While Vaca Diez and Fred were preparing for the journey upriver, Lizzie had time to write home; even to feel mildly homesick. To be sure, they had friends in Pará, mostly connected with rubber, such as Emilio Kanthack, the respected merchant and British Consul. He, like Fred, was a naturalised British citizen and had been in Pará for many years. But for Lizzie, nothing could replace a lively gossip with her own family.

She found Pará a very pretty town, with wide, tree-lined avenues, some grand buildings in the Portuguese style, and one of the largest theatres in South America – the Teatro do Paz. The construction of the theatre had begun in the days of the Brazilian Empire, long before the monarchy was overthrown in 1889. In March 1869 the foundation stone had been laid by the President of the province of Grão Pará, and nine years later the finest symbol of the city's prosperity was ready for inauguration. In other ways, too, Pará was well advanced, and Lizzie and Fred were able to ride on the trolleybus service of the Companhia Urbana de Estrada de Ferro Paraense. With foreign backing, the trolleys were being converted from horse traction to electricity, and such were the local interconnections between business and politics that the same company also gained a twenty-five-year contract to light the streets. As if warning Amazon speculators, however, the company's plans never fully got off the ground; Pará remained dark at night, while horses and steam kept the trolleys rolling.

Lizzie enjoyed Pará and was getting to like the climate.

New Hotel, Pará
18 January 1897

My dear Dad and Ma,

. . . Now I must tell you a little about Pará. We changed into the New Hotel yesterday, because our other room was too dirty and the W C we could not use at all. We had to pay a visit to one friend or another when we wanted to go, but this hotel is a new one and everything is kept clean.

We have two small beds with nets all the way round. Mine has some holes in it so my arms and hands are covered with bites, but last night Fred covered them up so I was all right. We have a nice shower bath too. You feel as if you must have a bath every morning. We get up about 7, it is too hot to stay in bed after, then we have our tea and rolls (no milk, we cannot get any, and the butter is awful).

Then Fred does his business and I amuse myself reading or writing my diary. At 10 or 11 we have our breakfast: it is really a hot dinner of 6 or 8 courses with plenty of nice wine and ice. After that we go out for a ride in the trams, which are open, or a walk. Then we go to sleep until 5 or 6, when we have our dinner. After dinner we go to a café or two.

I like the cooking here, but we do not get mutton more than once a week. All the meat is tough. We have paid one or two visits to English people here who live a little way out, but it is really too hot to go sight seeing. The heat agrees with me, I am glad to say. I feel quite well and my appetite is enormous.

In Lizzie's day British businessmen were already well established along the Amazon, and their spirit of enterprise, backed by the City of London, was forging ahead with shipping, railway projects, banking and public works of every description. One plan failed simply because of the power of the river: the British telegraph line started in 1895 to link Pará and Manaus, a fast-growing port 950 miles upriver, worked intermittently and at a loss because the riverbed on which it was laid changed every season. Amazon silting and currents could not be stopped or changed by any amount of capital.

As usual Lizzie, excluded like other ladies from all but the social aspects of the business world, found herself with time on her hands. She was also lonely because she had lost her pet.

> We brought Sambo to the hotel, but he has disappeared: all the doors are kept open so we suppose he ran out after another dog. They say we are sure to find him though, as there is not another like him in Pará.

Sadly Sambo, alias Bill Sikes, was never found. Her letter goes on to talk about other matters:

> I can only wear my thin cotton dresses here and I had even to take the collars off those, I could not bear them, and I had to buy some thin open shoes, you cannot wear closed ones.
>
> We get rain every day for a little while, also thunderstorms.
>
> I am very glad to get your letter and Bert's, which you wrote on Xmas Day. You came off well for presents. I only wish I could have been with you. We did not hear from anyone else. They must have posted their letters too late. I was disappointed I did not hear from Rosie. Now my dear Ma I must wish you a happy birthday as my next letter will arrive too late. I am sending you some little photos taken on the *Sobralense*, if they come in time. I shall think of you on your birthday and we will drink your health.
>
> We might by chance get your letter. It depends how long we stay here. Tell me the news and if you are all well.
>
> I have seen the cocoanuts and bananas growing, also lovely palm trees, but I am not allowed to eat it.

Considering the immense variety of tropical fruits in Pará, and their appeal, it seems odd that Lizzie was never tempted. The reason is not clear; most travellers peel a fruit as even washing water may be contaminated, but Lizzie perhaps felt that any fruit would make her bilious.

> Now give my love to everybody, also Fred's, and don't you forget us. We shall write from every port. You must write in about 2 months time to Orton. You can send every fortnight. Perhaps we shall get them all together, but that will be all the nicer.
>
> Now, goodbye, from your loving daughter,
> Lizzie

Then delay followed delay. Time in the Amazon meant nothing, even to the throng of hopeful fortune-seekers gathered along Pará's so-called Wall Street. Any businessman knew that negotiation demanded the careful priming of contacts: just the right pressure here, a nod there, a friendly slap on the arm at the port, or a few minutes at the state office to share a coffee. Pará trade was good: in the five years before Lizzie and Fred arrived rubber exports had more than doubled, and export taxes on these were up by over 400 per cent. A catalyst in this rapid growth was Pará's strategic position at the mouth of the river. However, there were rumours of political trouble ahead.

Politics always set Vaca Diez' adrenalin running – he had fled the Bolivian capital under the cloud of a political scandal, and now he sensed trouble in Pará. At the root of the problem was the rising temperature of competition between the state of Pará and its neighbour to the west, Amazonas, whose capital, Manaus, wanted more revenue. Manaus, or Manaos as it was then called, wanted to control all rubber exports from Amazonas and upriver. Certainly such Brazilian affairs should not have caused Vaca Diez any immediate alarm but he knew that his territory at Orton was close to the Brazilian border, behind a disputed boundary line; it was vulnerable should the Brazilians decide to move in. Vaca Diez had other problems, too, such as whom to trust in Brazil. Should he rely on Kanthack in Pará to be his agent, or should he follow Suárez, who was ready to open offices in both Manaus and Pará? He chose Kanthack, and continued preparing for the journey.

Soon after her arrival in Pará, Lizzie, who had apparently been looking forward to a little excitement, mentioned a change of plan:

I am disappointed to say that we are not going over the rapids.
Instead of taking the Madeira River, I think we are taking another
which takes longer but is much easier for travelling.

Any confusion in Lizzie's mind about the other river which she mentions is totally forgivable. Only sixteen years before the young couple left England, even the experts were still confused. Upriver on the Bolivian frontier a large section of land lay in limbo. The Beni River was known for some of its Bolivian course, but quite where it entered Brazil was a mystery. If one got on a raft and set off downstream the destination could be a surprise, and often was. Amazon pioneering usually entailed advancing either upstream from the main Amazon, or downstream from somewhere far inland.

The Madeira, a major tributary of the Amazon, is navigable upstream for about 500 miles until the way is blocked by a series of cataracts often called falls. The presence of over nineteen falls in 200 miles, and a drop of almost 300 feet, simply stops all progress on the river. Add to this the hazards of the hundreds of tons of fallen trees swept along by the current, which give the river its name, Madeira, meaning 'wood', and its notoriety is guaranteed.

In 1880 an American doctor called Edwin Heath found the link between the Beni River and the Madeira River, or Mamoré as it is known above the rapids. He even gave the Orton River its name, after his friend James Orton, an American university teacher who died before he could complete the Beni exploration. Heath also knew Vaca Diez and exchanged information with him; as one idea led to another, in due course Vaca Diez arrived on the Beni, eventually setting up his base near the mouth of the Orton River. But to rubber exporters the Madeira Falls remained a disaster area. To bypass the cataracts meant one of two unappealing choices. The rubber could be transported through the forest, which involved facing hostile Indians, or else every load had to be portaged across the falls, in which case the workforce became a sitting target for expert bowmen. It was hardly worth stopping to spin a coin. Despite everything the rubber was kept moving, but at tremendous cost. Steamers had to stop at San Antonio, the lowest of the falls. Above that point everything was shipped by a system of ferries or *batelãos* running in small fleets between each fall. This was the way Lizzie had described to 'Marie' of the *Morning Leader*, and believed they would take. However once in Pará Vaca Diez heard about an epidemic of yellow fever that was sweeping down the Madeira, hence the change of plan. After its treetrunks, the river was best known and most feared for its frequent outbreaks of that killer disease.

Any suggestion about a way to avoid the rapids was given top priority, as each time a *batelão* capsized – and they did so often – the lost rubber reduced the profit. The workers' lives were considered less important. One dream was a railway, and the first man to attempt the project was Colonel George E. Church, an American soldier who had fought in the Civil War. Church was also an accomplished explorer, geographer and engineer who quickly won the confidence of the Brazilian and Bolivian authorities with his plan to build a railway from below the lowest fall to above the highest one, a total distance of over 200 miles in fever-ridden country. Church, who was a Vice-President of the Royal Geographical Society of London, raised capital in England and found a British firm prepared to take on the job. The contractors set out for the Madeira in 1872, but a year later they had downed tools, despairing of the plan because of the appalling local conditions.

An American firm, Philip and Thomas Collins of Philadelphia, took up the challenge in 1877. A Brazilian commented, 'When the English came here, they did nothing but smoke and drink for two days – but the Americans work like the devil.' Devil or not, the Madeira jungle got the better of the Americans too. It was immensely thick jungle, broken only by swamps and deep gullies. Fever struck, and all around them Indians were watching and waiting for the right moment to attack and kill. Eventually the financing collapsed after mutinies and desertion by

31

the labour force and a scandal in Bolivia: when a government minister was buried alive by Indians in the Bolivian capital, or so it was said, confidence in the Bolivian securities and bonds supporting the scheme was undermined. P. and T. Collins went bankrupt, and the Madeira–Mamoré railway dream was put on ice.

Fred knew of the proposed rail route, which he marked on a sketch map sent to England with one of Lizzie's letters. He also marked the alternative river route, which had been discovered just three years before they left for Brazil. As Lizzie said, it was longer, but it had the advantage of being navigable for most of the way. The key to the route lay in two small tributaries close to the Andes, almost at the western limit of the Amazon network. A land crossing between the rivers meant that the Madeira system could be entered above the falls. The idea appealed to Vaca Diez, as it held the added attraction of opening up even more super-rich rubber lands. There was just one problem – he had to negotiate terms with a Peruvian called Carlos Fermín Fitzcarrald, the discoverer of the route. Fitzcarrald, the son of an American sailor who had married and settled in Peru, was noted for his fighting spirit; Vaca Diez expected tough talking and a hard bargain.

While Fred and Vaca Diez were planning in Pará, they heard some good news: the Peruvian Minister, Coronel Ibarra, had just granted Fitzcarrald exclusive navigation rights on the Ucayali River, the major waterway leading from the main Amazon to the new route. At the same time, though, Vaca Diez learnt that his competitor and cousin, Nicholás Suárez, who had returned to Bolivia, had beaten him and completed a deal with Fitzcarrald. The terms were vague, but it seemed that in return for using the route Suárez had offered Fitzcarrald rubber territory. Vaca Diez had no alternative but to go to Iquitos, a small town in Peru over 2000 miles up the Amazon, and negotiate with Fitzcarrald.

Lizzie, obviously delighted at being treated like a great lady, and as a result revealing certain traits of snobbishness which re-emerge from time to time, wrote home before their departure. She is clearly looking forward to the journey and wishes that her younger brother Bert, with his active and enquiring mind, could share it with them.

Hotel Central, Pará
18 January 1897

My dear Dad and Ma,
. . . Now I must tell you the way we are going to take. No one has been that way yet, so it will be very interesting. I only wish we could have had Bert with us, but I think there will be another expedition after we have safely arrived.

Above *Lizzie Hessel*

Inset *Fred Hessel*

Opposite above *A group photograph taken before Lizzie and Fred left for South America which includes three unnamed gentlemen. Back row: Ben Edwards on the left, Fred Hessel on the right. Lizzie centre front with sister Rose Edwards*

Opposite below *An earlier journey. From left to right: Ben Edwards, Rose, an unnamed friend, Lizzie and Fred*

Right *The interview with Lizzie by 'Marie' for the* Morning Leader *published in London on 29 December 1896 just before Lizzie left for South America*

WOMAN'S

HUNTING COSTUME FOR BOLIVIA.

AN ADVENTUROUS ENGLISHWOMAN

WHO WILL HELP TO OPEN UP AN UNKNOWN LAND

TELLS "MARIE" ABOUT HER PLANS, HER DANGERS, AND HER COSTUMES.

Where is Bolivia? I had to ask the question, for even I cannot be expected to know the exact location of every place on the surface of the earth. "Oh, I see, a large region in the west of South America. And who is going right up into the unexplored parts? The only white lady there? Excuse me." I was off to see her. She must have something new to tell.

In the train, of course, I pictured the lady as tall and muscular, with a masculine head, thick short hair, combed back from a high forehead, perhaps spectacles—anyway, large shoes and short skirts. "Surely," I thought, when I saw her in her charming drawing-room, "this tall, slight young girl, still under five-and-twenty, could not brave the dangers of unexplored lands." But it was so, and I plied my questions. The first naturally was "Are you not afraid to o all those thousands of miles and into such dangerous parts?"

"Oh, no, I am delighted. I shall like it, though unfortunately we shall meet with unpleasant weather nearly the whole time we are on our journey out. It will be eleven weeks before we reach the little settlement on the border of the unknown region to which we are going. My husband is to open up this country, and as he is to be away for five years or more I would not be left behind. We go up to Lisbon, via Paris, Bordeaux, Madrid, Lisbon, and Madeira, to Para, at the mouth of the Amazon. Here we shall probably meet our company of people numbering over 500. We all take river steamers—where we are to sleep on deck in hammocks—up the Amazon to the Madeira River, and change there for canoes. Our progress will be very slow after that, for each night we shall have to pitch camp on the ba— Here I must

expect I shall be very dull while my husband goes off up the country. He will be gone for about six weeks at a time and will have all kinds of dangers to encounter."

"Savage tribes?" I query.

"Yes. The tribes never exceed 40 or 50 though, and perhaps fortunately for us, they are always fighting among themselves. It is hardly likely that they have many firearms, but their

ARROWS ARE ALL POISON-TIPPED,

and they are expert marksmen."

"What about your outfit?" A woman's mind is never far from such affairs.

"Oh, come and see it.

This was what I wanted. I went with her and saw an enormous array of cool, pretty muslin, cotton, and zephyr dresses, one after another, spotted, flowered, striped, in white, cream, and all the coolest of pale tints; dressing and tea-gowns, and sunshades in dozens. White shoes, stockings, and gloves, sailor straws, Leghorn and Panama hats without end. I was astonded. "You see," said my hostess quietly, "they

HAVE TO LAST ME FIVE YEARS."

The petticoats and underclothing were beautiful, of the finest nainsook, Indian muslin, and web-like silk. Yet among them all were mixed flannel nightdresses, of a weight seldom worn during an English winter. "The nights are treacherous," explained my hostess, "and these, you see, she added, "are my hunting outfit.

Long brown boots fitting to the shape of the leg, laced up in front almost to touch the knee. Then light brown and fawn riding knickers of the thinnest materials, buttoned and buckled just below the knee and at the back of a shaped waistband. Ordinary loose cotton shirt blouses are worn with these, and light ties supply the finishing touch. The head is crowned with a large hat, the spre— the better. belt with

Above *A family garden scene. From left to right: John (Jack) Edwards, Rose, an unnamed friend, Fred and Lizzie. Barry the dog is in the foreground*

Below *Pará – now Belém – at the mouth of the Amazon. Fred and Lizzie arrived here early in January 1897*

A mangrove tree on Marajó
Island in the mouth of the Amazon.
This island, the size of Switzerland,
would have been on Lizzie's right as she
entered the river by steamer

Opposite above *The Rio Negro, a tributary of the Amazon*

Opposite below *Well-constructed houses were the mark of success, and foreign companies working in the Amazon during the rubber boom built to last*

Above *First-class travel on the Amazon in the 1880s*

Right *A Machiguenga Indian girl of the Urubamba River cleaning cocoa beans. These Indians were taken as slaves by the rubber gatherers, and the practice continued well into this century*

Before the Madeira–Mamoré railway was built, heavy canoes and batalãos had to be pulled on rollers through the forests beside the Madeira rapids. It was on a journey like this that Gregorio Suárez was killed by Indians in 1904. Teams of up to fifteen men were engaged permanently for this work

Well, the next steamer which we take from here is called the *Rio Branco*, one of the Amazon steamers. She is very large and all the cabins are on deck, also we dine on deck. They took me over her so that I could choose my cabin; I can tell you I come first in everything. The French lady is the wife of a man who takes a very small position, so they do not study her. Well, Fred and I have a cabin for four all to ourselves, so we have plenty of room; then there is a lovely shower bath, also proper WC (which is a grand thing for this country) for us 2 ladies only. We shall be 25 1st class passengers; the others will not be allowed up on deck. If they attempt to come up they will be shot. Everyone is armed to be on the safe side. Well, our first stopping place will be Manaos. We do not stop there more than 2 days, then we go on to Iquitos in Peru, where we have to leave the steamer and wait while they put the launches together, which will take at least 6 weeks. From there the emigrants travel in canoes, we in the launches. From Iquitos we go up the Ucayali and Urubamba then we have to cut our way through the forest for 5 days, till we come to the river Madre de Dios, which takes us to the Beni River where the reason we could not take the Madeira River is, they say, the Indians have poisoned the whole of the river so it is not possible to use it.

Lizzie's idea that the river had been poisoned was probably just a misunderstanding of a local expression for a bad river. News that the yellow fever epidemic had blanketed the Madeira finally convinced Vaca Diez to use Fitzcarrald's route, and towards the end of January 1897 he was ready to move; he needed only one more message to assure him that every part of his plan was in place. On 1 February 1897, news came from London to say that registration of his company was going ahead. As Consul-General, Francisco Suárez had been given the power of attorney to act for Vaca Diez. The Banque Française de l'Afrique du Sud had taken up 10,000 ordinary shares; the work in Paris had paid off. The new company's papers listed the assets: 4278 *estradas* (paths) through the forest, passing approximately 150 rubber trees each – 2878 on the Orton River, 900 on the Tahuamanu River (a tributary of the Orton), and 500 on the Beni. Thousands of tons of rubber now belonged to the London company, and all the profits could be kept in Europe.

The next day Vaca Diez, Fred and Lizzie set out upstream on the Amazon steamer *Rio Branco*, taking with them two dismantled steam launches, an arsenal of weapons, and several tons of supplies including champagne, wine and perfume. With them travelled four Germans, two engineers and two clerks, 'well educated and real gentlemen', as Lizzie described them; a French lady, the wife of one of the clerks; 180 immigrants, possibly hijacked from Pará; and a large dog belonging to Vaca Diez – useful as fresh meat or for keeping hostile Indians at bay.

Chapter Three

'Champagne on ice and a phonograph all included'

Rio Branco, Amazon River
8 February 1897

My dear Dad and Mum,

We are steaming along in the Amazon River and have been for the last week. The weather is very hot but always a little breeze. I must begin at the beginning and tell you everything I can think about.

They entered the Narrows one day above Pará. There, in a maze of a thousand forested islands, the channel leads west of Marajó, an island the size of Switzerland. Rich tropical vegetation closed around the *Rio Branco* and at the tight bend of Furo Grande the jungle, brushing the bow and stern, littered the deck. Massive trees, some rearing majestically to over 100 feet, lined the bank.

The scenery is grand, though it is all forest. The trees are a tremendous height; it is all green with palms, creepers, etc., no flowers at all. We have passed several native huts occupied by Indians. They are made of wood and mud and the roofs are of palm leaves; some of them have no walls at all, just the foundation and roof; they seem to have no furniture except hammocks.

Lizzie, always fond of animals, was fascinated by the natural history of the river: 'We have seen two alligators already,' she wrote, 'several garcias and pheasants.' She probably meant caimans, the South American crocodilian, herons, and the curious hoatzin, a pheasant-sized brown bird and weak flier which lives close to water. Lizzie was homesick now and possibly starting to be apprehensive of the journey ahead.

I feel the want of a companion badly and, had we known how the expedition was to be arranged, we should have brought Bert along if he would have been satisfied with a small salary. There are people from all nations and they arrange themselves into the corners of the ship, all the Germans together etc., and then there is a great deal of jealousy going on. We have three Englishmen but they are only second class passengers so I must not talk to them much. I have to think of my position. I have slept in the hammock every night and quite like it now; you have to know just how to get in, then it is quite as comfortable as a bed.

Once into the main Amazon streamway, boats keep away from the bank. It is then that the size of the river seems impressive for the first time. Fresh water stretches to the horizon, muddy brown and broken only by rafts of floating grass and mauve-flowered water hyacinths.

Two days later and halfway to Manaus, they passed the mouth of the Tapajós River on their port bow. The Tapajós begins life over 1000 miles away in the Mato Grosso of West Brazil and flows north to the Amazon as a blue stream. Where the two rivers meet, the different waters, one turbid, the other clear, swirl downriver side by side for many miles until eventually they commingle. Backed by low hills on the distant southern bank at the confluence, the quiet town of Santarém is a monument to the history of rubber. Lizzie never mentioned Santarém, and she probably had heard only scraps of information, if that, about Henry Alexander Wickham, who had established himself there soon after she was born.

Wickham was one of that curious breed of extraordinarily vague mid-nineteenth-century travellers. The son of a London solicitor, he was a pioneer dedicated to travelling. He grew up with no particular ambition, and arrived in the Amazon by way of Nicaragua and Venezuela, finally settling with his wife and mother in Santarém, where he tried to live in much the same way as the locals, building himself a house and farming. Wickham found himself in the right place at the right time. Back in London, the Royal Botanic Gardens at Kew needed rubber seeds – not just any rubber seeds, but the best. Rubber in the London market had already begun to be graded, and certain types fetched higher prices. 'Old dry fine Pará' made the best price, and Victorian empire builders saw the advantages of transferring rubber seed to Ceylon (now Sri Lanka) and Malaya, then British possessions, and producing latex there.

For Wickham, a self-taught plant collector, collecting represented a way to finance his pioneering way of life. With the authority of the India Office in London, under whose jurisdiction Ceylon and Malaya fell, Dr Joseph Hooker, Director of Kew, commissioned Wickham to collect 10,000 or more seeds. Not much was known about rubber botany, though the trees were recognised easily by the tappers and traders. One species, *Hevea brasiliensis*, could be tapped for twenty-five years or more without apparent damage; another, *Castilloa elastica*, was destroyed by tapping.

Hooker needed *Hevea* seeds and he got them. By sheer hard work and good fortune Wickham collected 90,000 seeds, packed them in banana leaves and despatched them on a British ship to Liverpool. By the time Lizzie passed Santarém *Hevea* trees had been growing in Ceylon for twenty years, and the first Malayan plantation rubber was being sold in London. It marked the beginning of a price war.

Lizzie seems to have adapted to life on the *Rio Branco* – not surprisingly, since with Vaca Diez' patronage she received special attention.

In the first place we are both quite well and I am always hungry.

We live very well dining with Mr Vaca Diez at a small table, just the six special people, so we have the best of everything, wine included; the others are not satisfied with their food and get no wine unless they pay for it.

The key to money, position and power in the Amazon was territory, and territory was counted in *estradas* of rubber trees; thereafter the economics were simple. Labourers, known as *seringueiros* after *seringueira*, a local name for the rubber tree, stayed in the forest tapping or making cuts to drain the latex. A *seringueiro* was given a contract to produce a certain quantity of crude rubber, which he did by smoking the latex over a fire of smouldering oily nuts from various palms. The best of these nuts, the *inaja*, were hard to find, so the *seringueiros* commonly used *uricuri* nuts, which were as large as a small hen's egg, solid and full of fuel. To make a large ball, a *pelle* or *bolacha*, of rubber, raw latex was dripped on a pole turned in the smoke. Production details varied from place to place and so did the contracts, though the result was the same: a *seringueiro* was always in debt – not through his own bad management, but because he was tied by contract to a system he could not beat.

When he delivered rubber to the owner of the *estradas*, the *seringalista* or *patrón*, usually at a collecting point along the river, the *seringueiro* was credited with an amount of money which was often far less than 50 per cent of the current market value of what he had produced. Hollow excuses still familiar today sought to justify the bad price – transport costs, insurance losses and overheads, rising all the time. . . . The *seringueiro* came to expect a low return and a sad existence alone, or with his poorly fed wife and children, on an isolated *estrada*. Towns were non-existent on the remote 'rubber rivers' and settlements were few and far between, so the *seringueiro* was obliged to buy his food, clothes, Winchester rifle and cartridges, supplies for his family – indeed everything he needed – from the *seringalista*. Purchases were marked in the accounts book, often with 20 per cent added as commission, even though Amazon prices were already high. Day by day the *seringueiro* found himself deeper in debt. With a wet season of several months, during which he could not produce, a *seringueiro*'s debt crisis often reached breaking point. One turn-of-the-century estimate held that every ton of rubber cost two poorly paid lives, and without such a low production cost there would never have been a profit. Nor could a *seringueiro* escape and lose himself in the Amazon, for *seringalistas* usually employed armed guards to follow and bring back any fleeing *seringueiro*. Guard posts on rivers were normal, not only to prevent workers from getting out, but to deter unauthorised visitors from snooping. Outsiders were unwelcome in the lawless rubber lands.

Some of the hazards of the jungle environment now began to impinge a little on Lizzie's awareness:

> We had a nasty little occurrence a few days ago. One of the Spaniards had been drinking very much in Pará and it brought on fever. He died on board at 4 o'clock in the morning and the same morning the ship was stopped and they rowed him ashore and buried him; he was put into a rough coffin and they also made him a cross on which they put his name. There are also three women ill with fever amongst the emigrants, but I don't wonder at it, they are packed like a lot of cattle down below and the smell is dreadful.

Soon afterwards the *Rio Branco* altered course to avoid the currents where the Madeira entered on the port bow. The gentle swish of the water and soft hiss of the steam engine hardly altered pace. Nine hundred miles upriver, the Amazon is pushed aside by the clear, tea-coloured water of the Rio Negro. Lizzie saw signs of a large town ahead: settlements on the banks with thatched huts, cows and the smell of wood smoke meant civilisation again. Soon after breakfast, keeping to the right bank of the river, they headed into the Rio Negro.

> I am sure I don't know when we shall reach Orton, we are going along so slowly. This morning . . . we hope to reach Manaos where we shall stop for a day. We are going ashore but the others will not be allowed to.

Riverboats carrying immigrants often kept well offshore in Manaus, to prevent them jumping ship. By the time they had reached this point in their journey, the recruits must have guessed the fate in store for them upriver. Many tried to flee before it was too late, but Manaus would not have offered them much – it was a place for the rich.

Either one of Lizzie's letters is missing, or perhaps she never went ashore. On the other hand, she may have closed her eyes to the extravagant scene and decided not to say anything. Manaus was the glittering centre of the Amazon, a city where vast sums were spent and forgotten as the local rubber barons indulged their fantasies. Unlike

Suárez and Vaca Diez, who lived at their holdings, most rubber barons kept to the city, relying on managers and a trusted chain of command reaching into the forest.

Even as the *Rio Branco* lay in the harbour Lizzie must have glanced at the massive shape of the Teatro Amazonas, which dominated the city's skyline; gold, green and blue tiles – the national colours of Brazil – covered its dome. The theatre, known always to the British as the Opera House, had been inaugurated in December 1896, and the first performance had been presented only a month before Lizzie and Fred arrived. A dream of the Governor, Eduardo Ribeiro, the building had cost the equivalent of two million dollars – a lavish undertaking in tune with the spirit of Manaus. Ironwork had been shipped from Glasgow, marble from Italy, mirrors, chandeliers and the finest Sèvres porcelain from France, and hand-carved furniture from London. Artists were commissioned to decorate the walls, ceilings and stage curtain.

On 6 January 1897 the *Diario Official*, the most important newspaper in Manaus, announced that Ponchielli's opera *La Gioconda* was to be performed by the Grande Companhia Lirica Italiana on the following day. The conductor was Enrico Bernardi, Gioconda was Libia Drog, and La Greca was to be sung by A. Tumugalti. Like many important occasions in Manaus, the evening's entertainment had been organised by an impresario, this time Joaquim de Carvalho Franco, who by 10 February, when Lizzie was there, was asking the government for certain expenses. Wrangles were also continuing about payments for the final construction work, and accounts were being argued with J. C. Ferreira Villas Boas for coal brought from Cardiff to power the electrical generators. After many years of stop-go planning and finance, the Teatro Amazonas began its working life with a bump. Many tales of triumph are told about splendid, glittering performances: most are without foundation, and certainly Caruso and Bernhardt never performed at this extraordinary white elephant.

The rich and powerful in Manaus dressed in the finest European fashions and used money as if its possession were an embarrassment to them. Diamonds and gold were openly traded as the preferred currency. One madam ran a gilded floating bordello housing the most alluring Brazilian girls and offering 'Frequent sailings to all parts of the river – champagne on ice and a phonograph all included'. Manaus parties had to be wild to make news, so a bath filled with gallons of the best French champagne and a naked Polish Jewess is a story of doubtful but lasting value – possibly because it has all the right elements. Polish Jewesses were the favoured mistresses of the wealthy men of Manaus, and champagne was an easily acquired taste. At two dollars a bottle it was consumed at every opportunity – and from a beautifully warmed bath, or so it is said. Nothing was surprising in Manaus, and a report that more than 60 per cent of the residences were brothels never raised an eyebrow.

Fred may have been reluctant to leave the city, with its obvious potential for business. Trade was always brisk, and new stores were opening every day. A floating harbour had been built to accommodate the annual 45-foot rise and fall of the Rio Negro – not a tide, simply the effect of a tropical rainy season. The concession for the work was granted originally to a Polish nobleman, Baron Rymkievicz, and a Cuban engineer, Señor Lavendeyra, who found support in the Booth Steamship Co., a British firm. Manaus lagged behind Pará in trams, a telegraph and telephone system, and banking; but the situation was not to last for long, as the upriver rubber lands were the richest yet.

The *Rio Branco*, with Fred and Lizzie on board, now moved on towards the uncompromising forests that were fuelling the growing boom. Their next stop was Iquitos, 1000 miles upstream. From the Rio Negro the steamer turned back into the Amazon or Solimões, as the Portuguese named the next part of the river. The river is wide and in February it begins its annual flood, spreading high over the banks and inundating millions of square miles of forest. The few settlements where the *Rio Branco* stopped were on marginally higher ground. Lizzie's last letter before they reached Peru ended:

Yesterday we stopped to take cattle from a small farm; it was amusing. They tie ropes on to the horns of the bullock, then hunt him into the water; then he has to swim to the ship; some of them gave a great deal of trouble and very often, the men had to run.

Now goodbye for the next two weeks, when I shall write from Iquitos: think of me steaming along. With love to all from Fred and myself.

Your loving daughter
Lizzie

More rivers enter on the right. The largest of them, the Japurá, the Putumayo and the Napo, begin in the snows of the Andes of Colombia and Ecuador. The Putumayo flows through the forests of abundant *Castilloa* in a region where borders were ill defined in Lizzie's day. Frontier disputes were daily talk and everywhere unresolved; a no man's land waited for anybody who had the courage to take it. Nothing, not even a yard of forest, was secure, and commercial interests invariably transcended national boundaries. Iquitos, their destination, was the centre of many disputes. Earlier it had been known as Ecuadorian, but by Lizzie's time Peru was claiming it. Being far upriver on the one hand, and cut off from the Pacific by the Andes on the other, Iquitos was like the end of the Earth. Britain was not officially represented there, so Lizzie and Fred were guests of the German business house of Wesche.

Wesche & Co., German Consulate, Iquitos, Peru

12 March 1897

My dear Dad and Mama,

We have been here in Iquitos quite safe and well for the last three weeks. We are staying at the only nice house in the town belonging to a Mr Weiss, a German bachelor, to whom we had a letter of introduction; he sent someone on board the *Rio Branco* to fetch us, and we are his guests for six months if we like to stay. There is a German lady housekeeper who is very nice and she speaks English fairly well, so I have a companion: then there are twelve clerks who live in the house also, so we are a large family.

The other people of the expedition have a house in the town, but it is not furnished; they have to manage as best they can with their hammocks etc. More than three-quarters of the emigrants have deserted so we are taking Indians from upriver if we can get them. So far only two people have died and that was through their own carelessness at the different villages where we stopped for fuel. They all went ashore and brought back unripe fruit which gave them fever. They are a reckless lot, these Spaniards, and we are surprised that more of them have not been ill.

The journey from Pará to Iquitos by an ordinary steamer takes only 18 days but we were exactly four weeks over it. We had two lighters to tug and sometimes we stopped twice a day for fuel at small villages. We had no real trouble with the emigrants but they were always threatening to shoot the six of us who dined at the special table because they were not fed properly. Every night we had two sentinels at the staircases, armed with rifles and pistols, but nothing happened; they make a great deal of noise but they are cowards. We were made as comfortable as possible on the steamer, but after the first two weeks the journey was monotonous. The country also saw several parrots, pheasants and garcias.

Present-day Iquitos is peopled by a wide range of races and nationalities, more so than anywhere else on the Amazon. Not just one Chinese restaurant wafts a tempting smell of Wantun Frito on to the street, but dozens. The faces of light-skinned forest Indians blend with the darker bronze of *mestizos* from the Andes. Turks, Lebanese, Syrians, wartime European refugees, Americans both white and negro – half the world seems to be washed up in Iquitos. As long as twenty-four years before Lizzie was there James Orton had said, 'It now numbers 2000, English, Americans, Portuguese, Peruvians, Indians and nondescripts, the last forming a numerous class.'

The main part of the city stands well above the river, which is why the site was first chosen for a settlement by the Jesuits in 1739. Without the bank the town would be underwater; indeed, much of it is anyway, in a flood season when the river rises 30 feet. Floods have caused the bank to collapse, and parts of the waterfront street or Malecón hang in mid-air, waiting to plunge Amazonwards. Apart from its muddy pedestal, Iquitos seems at first sight to be badly placed, as it is over 120 miles downstream from the confluence of two impressive tributaries, the Ucayali and the Marañon – at one time the Amazon passing Iquitos was itself called the Marañon. Only at low water, during July and August, can Iquitos stand high, so when Lizzie arrived in February 1897 the *Rio Branco* could have steamed almost into the main street.

Iquitos had fewer than 6000 inhabitants at this time, and though its fortunes were improving its prosperity still lay a long way in the future. Orton had remarked:

> In Iquitos are to be found seventy or eighty Englishmen, who are employees in the public workshops, some of them having their families with them, and they form the largest body of Anglo-Saxons on the whole length of the Marañon – an occasional Yankee, who, by-the-bye, does not appear in this district to be much of a developer of ideas – and a German here and there seems to be looking for a good opening, as also is the stray Frenchman.

Lizzie, however, never mentioned meeting any compatriots, however, and the steamer may simply have moved on upriver. The presence of British people in the Amazon at this time was an indication of money, or certainly of the prospect of making it. The principal interests in the early days were cinchona bark, for the extraction of quinine, and riverboat engineering, which was a flourishing trade, especially for British engineers.

When Lizzie and Fred arrived, not much about the town was new, and she described it in these words:

> Iquitos is a very small town and it lies at the back of a bay, so the view from my window is very pretty; there is the forest on either side and the river right in front. Since I have been here I have only been out twice and that was only to go across to the English steamer *Huaskar* for breakfast. The people do not think of going

for walks; the house is large and there is also a long verandah where we promenade.

A more observant account, or perhaps one not doctored for the benefit of a family back in England, was that of a turn-of-the-century British traveller, Joseph Woodroffe, who spent a month in the town without the protection of the comforts provided by Mr Weiss. The lodging houses were mean and dirty, kerosene lamps smoked at night, and all day the streets were filled with a cacophony of noise and scavenging animals. Woodroffe wrote of 'open drains, vultures, and pigs in the street feeding on rubbish. Sanitary arrangements virtually unknown except where a few foreigners had erected rude structures over deep holes in the ground.' Around the homes were piles of refuse 'consisting for the most part of empty tin cans, broken bottles, crockery and the usual refuse from the kitchen'. In this mess 'fowls scratched all day and dirty ducks waddled in puddles of dirty water thrown from the kitchen'. There was no drinking water except 'that to be bought from water carriers in the streets', and even that transaction was risky, as one could be hit by the contents of a chamber pot thrown into the street from some door or window. Going for a walk was not popular, Lizzie had said, and one can see why.

The Amazon was opened to international navigation by imperial Brazilian decree in 1866. At first only a few ships ventured upriver, but trade and shipping improved quickly. After Pará and Manaus, Iquitos became the British upriver target, and the *Huascar* (or *Huaskar*, as Lizzie spelt it), a tiny vessel of only 960 tons, was one of the first British ships to get there direct from England. While Lizzie was waiting for Fred and Vaca Diez to complete their preparations for the next stage, she made the acquaintance of James Good, the *Huascar*'s captain.

They are running direct steamers from Liverpool to Iquitos now. The first one was the *Huaskar* with Captain Good, a very nice man. He has just this minute sent me over some mince pies. I told him I liked cakes so every few days he sends me something nice; we always take breakfast, or lunch rather, with him on Sundays. Bert must come on his steamer if we can arrange it.

[Iquitos]
29 March [1897]

My dear Dad and Mama,

Since I wrote you last I have been very gay. On the 19th I went to a ball on board the *Huaskar*. It was the Captain's birthday, the ship was decorated beautifully with flags and Chinese lanterns. At 9 o'clock I opened the ball with the Captain and I danced every

dance until 1 o'clock. We enjoyed ourselves very much; it was a
nice change in our now quiet lives.

Among the mementoes which Lizzie sent home was a calling card from
Captain Good with an invitation, printed in Spanish and addressed to
'Señor Fred Hessel and Señora', to visit his ship on Friday 19 March to
take tea.

Wesche was the main trading house in Iquitos and every rubber
business needed the Wesche credit and overseas connections. Iquitos
was known at the time for two reasons: it was expensive and it was
isolated, and such basic commodities as tinned butter and eggs were
scarce and overpriced. To offset these hardships almost anything could
be exchanged for rubber, even grandmothers – though they were not
worth as much as the *mujeres frescas*, the young Indian girls from the
forest.

Soon after her arrival Lizzie mentioned 'Indians from upriver', and
clearly Vaca Diez was facing a labour shortage. In another letter she also
referred to 500 Japanese emigrants which they were expecting to have
sent out. Moving people around the world was nothing new: the
antecedents of the Chinese in present-day Iquitos arrived in Peru with
the coolie trade out of Macao, mostly between 1861 and 1875. They
came as labourers to work on the land and engineering projects, including railways. Contracts were tough:

> It is solemnly declared in the present contract that I, Chie Lom,
> have freely and spontaneously agreed with Don —— to embark on
> the Italian bark [ship] with the object of going to Peru – and I bind
> myself as soon as I arrive to place myself at the orders of the before
> mentioned gentleman . . . to serve . . . for 8 years.

The outward fare was paid by the Peruvian employer, who offered a few
expenses and three days' holiday a year for religious festivals. Debts had
to be paid off by work, and the fare home was not covered. It is an old
saying in South America that if a contract is needed, the local jobbing
printer will run off a few copies, with no questions asked and all
government stamps included. Printers must have made good money
with contracts for labour at this period.

Apart from immigrants from overseas, native South Americans also
formed part of the workforce. The *flagelados*, a name for the 'scourged'
people of Ceará – Brazil's arid, impoverished northeast – flocked to the
Amazon during the great droughts of 1877 and 1888. Anything was
better than starvation at home, or so they thought. Some were so
desperate and dehumanised that they even ventured beyond Iquitos.
Lizzie described the 'local' people:

The Peruvians are very much like the Indians, with yellow skins, black hair and eyes; most of them go about barefooted. The way the men work is wonderful. They load them like animals, tremendous luggage they carry on their backs, first tied round the forehead with a webbing band; my big trunks one man carried upstairs in that way.

Julio César Arana, an able Peruvian, was to make history. The son of a hatmaker in the tiny town of Rioja in the Andean foothills, Arana first moved to Yurimaguas on the Huallaga River, a tributary of the Marañon, where he learnt the rubber business the hard way. He traded, made enemies, money and decisions until eventually, in 1886, at the age of thirty-two, he settled in Iquitos. Arana prospered first as Arana Hermanos, then as the Peruvian Amazon Rubber Co., and finally as the Peruvian Amazon Rubber Co. Ltd, floated in London, with a capital of one million pounds.

Lizzie never mentioned Arana, though in a place as small as Iquitos he would not have missed her arrival. An expedition led by a competitor such as Vaca Diez on the *Rio Branco* would have set the Iquiteños gossiping for weeks. Vaca Diez clearly meant business, and even if his destination was Bolivia Arana hated competition.

Fred and Lizzie stayed in Iquitos for almost three months, guests of the hospitable Mr Weiss. Vaca Diez went upriver, leaving Fred in charge. Lizzie was thrilled at the implications.

Mr Vaca Diez has gone up river for a week or so and has given Fred full power, so we are alright. We are the most fortunate people of the expedition: we do everything and have everything we like. Mr Vaca Diez has taken quite a fancy to Fred.

Now I must tell you how I spend my days. At 6 o'clock we get up and take a shower bath, then we take our coffee. Fred goes off to superintend things and I have been unpacking our trunks. The climate is so damp here everything has to be put in the sun every few weeks; we also have to sleep in our blankets. At 11 o'clock we have our breakfast, which is really a dinner, but very often for a whole week we cannot get fresh meat, we have to live on tinned meats and vegetables; but we have plenty of nice wine which makes up for it.

After breakfast we take coffee in the drawing room, then comes a nice siesta of a couple of hours, then I dress for dinner at $\frac{1}{2}$ past 5; after dinner we have music or promenade, drinks and then to bed at 9 o'clock. Everyone takes life easily; there is no hurrying and making ends meet and they are all so hospitable. We are here for as long as we like to stay in a beautiful bedroom and everything of the best. No paying for it: we are guests. Now I think I have nothing else to say, except that I would like to pay you a visit.

Today we had 96 degrees. The mosquitos here are terrible, but I have learnt the knack of catching them. Please let Rosie [Lizzie's sister] read this as I have not her address, and give my love to everyone.

With best love to you both from Fred and myself,
Lizzie

Making money – the aim of the whole expedition – was never far from their minds.

I am afraid we take life so easily in these countries. We must make our fortunes before we settle down in London again, so that we can take it easy there too. The mosquitos here are dreadful, I have to wear two pairs of stockings.

With half a million rubber trees awaiting them around Orton, the future seemed assured.

Chapter Four

'I have . . . given up corsets altogether'

Vaca Diez expected to find Nicholás Suárez and Fitzcarrald in Iquitos, but according to Lizzie the meeting never took place. Fitzcarrald was out of town some thousand miles upriver, and Suárez was at one of his *barracas* or control centres on the Bolivian frontier. Luckily, Vaca Diez found a friend in Wesche, for problems were piling in from every direction. Back in London Francisco Suárez had died in early February, aged sixty-four, intestate and leaving some £74,000 and his house in Compayne Gardens, Hampstead. He had been holding Vaca Diez' power of attorney, virtually controlling the company and its cash resources. Then, in Iquitos, the Customs were being troublesome, as Lizzie had mentioned on 12 March soon after their arrival.

> Our launches are getting along very slowly, we have to wait
> about so for the Customs House people. We expect to be here
> another two weeks.

Life was unpredictable and therefore exciting.

> . . . then will come the best part of the journey; we have met
> several people here who have been part of the way, and they say it
> is a most beautiful and interesting journey, but it will take us
> another four months from here to Orton.

Any rubber *patrón* found a boat or boats essential, so that he could collect the heavy *bolachas* or balls of rubber from his holdings along the river. Two small, dismantled, iron-hulled launches already accompanied the expedition, and when Suárez and Fitzcarrald joined forces to exploit the new route in the river maze beyond the Ucayali Suárez immediately ordered two small steamers. One, the *Bermudez*, he bought in Iquitos, and the other, the *Union*, a *lancha* – a small steam launch with a roof and a tall funnel – he ordered from Europe. The launches brought to Iquitos by Vaca Diez were the five-ton *Cintra* and the eight-ton *Adolfito*. Vaca Diez also purchased a small tug, the *Bolivar*; at Orton, ready and waiting for his arrival, he had another, the *Sernamby*. This flotilla was not just a status symbol – many merchants in Pará kept a larger number of boats – but Vaca Diez, Suárez and Fitzcarrald were determined to control a network of waterways which, if unravelled, would stretch from London to New York.

Planning such an advance kept Vaca Diez and Fred tied up for almost three months, and the delay gave Lizzie plenty of time to write and receive letters from home.

Last Saturday we had a party here at the house. Mr Weiss was godfather to his partner's child and the Baptism was held here at the house. We had dancing and singing and plenty of champagne. The ladies were presented with small flowers as souvenirs (I send you mine), and the gentlemen with coins tied with ribbon.

By late March some progress had been made. The launches were on the river, though not without their problems. Vaca Diez soon discovered that as a man with money he was expected to pay top prices. He certainly did not want a large boat on the Ucayali until he knew the terms of his deal with Fitzcarrald. Lizzie was aware of these difficulties to a certain extent:

We have been here five weeks next Wednesday and we do not know yet when we shall get away. We are trying to hire a launch, the *Laura*, but I think they will only sell her. She is much larger than ours and is more comfortable altogether. I went for a trial trip in one of our launches and the boiler ran short of water. We were drifting for 1 hour and a half whilst they filled it again and got up steam. The people were frightened and sent all round the town to know if we had come back and they were just steaming after us when we came along. No more trial trips for me; as soon as the boat stops the mosquitos simply come and eat you up.

Her letters continued, some containing everyday details: 'We have had several storms too' . . . 'We are expecting a steamer in today with the European mails: there was one in last week but there was no news.' Sometimes she mentions their plans: 'We are taking an English doctor up with us. He is very nice and will be a companion for us; he met us here in Iquitos but Fred engaged him in Pará.'

By mid-April cooler, drier weather was coming up from the south. They were still in Iquitos, and although Lizzie never suggested it, the delay was probably engineered by the local people in order to tie up Vaca Diez. The river begins to fall quickly after April, resulting in slower travel and more expense for the launches.

German Consul, Iquitos, Peru
Wednesday, 14 April 1897

My dear Dad and Mama,

We are still here in Iquitos and both of us in very good health. My appetite is still enormous and I have gained five pounds in weight.

We hope to get away this day week in the *Laura*, a nice little launch belonging to Mr Weiss, the gentleman with whom we are staying; she has no cabin though, but they are going to make me a tarpaulin screen where I can dress myself, etc. She has two decks, the upper one we shall have with Vaca Diez and 2 or 3 others, the lower one is for the other people. And then we are taking our two small steam launches.

Their destination lay over 1000 river miles from Iquitos, among shallow tributaries. The route discovered by Fitzcarrald was new ground for Vaca Diez and, although many Peruvian rivermen knew the Ucayali, the rivers leading into it in the higher reaches were a different matter. Fitzcarrald's route had been tried only twice and, while being navigable most of the way, a short portage through forest was involved – all the cargo would have to be unloaded and carried between the rivers, so Vaca Diez was advised to sell many of the goods brought from Europe. Fred and Vaca Diez made a deal with Fitzcarrald's partner: they had to trust him with the boxes and crates holding thousands of pounds' worth of stock, much of it consisting of European luxuries. In the end they put some of their own party in charge, Lizzie explained.

Most of our cargo is to be left here and they have arranged a shop where they will sell it. Two or three of our people will stay here in charge. It is a pity we cannot take it all with us because they are all goods we should be glad to have in Orton, but it is impossible the way we are going to take much cargo.

Last Saturday until Monday we went for a trip in one of Mr Weiss's boats, as far as the Ucayali; all the gentlemen of the house, Fred and I and the English Doctor. We went first to Puritana, a small village where they have a saw mill. But the mosquitos were so terrible that we only stayed a few hours. They have some very fine machinery for cutting the wood, but the houses and the Indians were very wretched, how they manage to keep strong I do not know. The Indians live on a root called *euchre* like a potato and cooked bananas they eat, but the way they work is wonderful. We then went higher up to a village where they make *Cachace*: it is a spirit made from sugar cane and very strong. There we stayed for a few hours. We went ashore in canoes. It is a very prosperous village, also some fine cattle and any amount of pigs which live on the waste sugar cane.

We had our meals on the boat and also slept in hammocks on the boat, but under nets for there were swarms of mosquitos. We enjoyed ourselves very much and wish you could all have come

49

with us to see the country and the queer people, some of them are just like animals.

It had not taken long for Lizzie to pick up the custom of believing that the Indians were not people. To the locals, it was no more than an expression of social superiority acquired from three centuries of European domination. Commonly heard in the Spanish Amazon countries, even in recent years, was the remark '*No son gente, son animales*' . . . 'They're not people, they're animals.'

From Iquitos onwards Lizzie's letters were punctuated by comments about Indians or 'savages' – not her personal view, and again the local term for '*salvajes*' or 'wild' forest Indians who had had little or no contact with civilisation. The *euchre* mentioned several times was certainly *yuca*, the wild sweet manioc, usually boiled and then sometimes fried as well. Her *Cachace* was *cachaça*, the Brazilian name for a near-pure alcohol distilled from sugar cane, and the use of the Brazilian name is a measure of Brazilian influence across the Amazon at the time. The same spirit is sold in Peru today as *aguardiente*.

On the 17th they were still in Iquitos and Lizzie decided to write to Nell. New pets had to substitute for her family, and she told her sister of these animal friends. Bib was Lizzie's sister Edith, only eighteen when Lizzie and Fred set out, and as Nell remembered 'a strong character'. Lizzie clearly had no intention of letting distance, even across the Amazon, keep her apart from the Mathys family.

Iquitos, Peru
17 April 1897

My dear Nellie,

I was very pleased to get your letter and to hear all about your Xmas and your birthday. You did have a lot of nice things. I wish I had been there to hang up my stocking, but I was in Lisbon on Xmas day. Tell Bib she is very good to write such long letters to Orton and I also hope she is enjoying all the dances. She must have looked nice in her new dress. I must tell you it is not very easy to write here, for the mosquitos are after my hands, the flies are buzzing around my head and a wasp building his nest on top of my looking glass; also some ants carrying a beetle along to their nest, so I have enough to do to look after all those things.

I am pleased to know that my Polly is being spoilt and also that your Kitty is well again. I will send you photos of my new family when I am in Orton. We did not find Bill Sikes again, he must have been stolen, but our doctor has a dog and Mr Vaca Diez has two large ones, so I have something to go silly over now and again.

You must learn as much as you can whilst you are at school. It was good to hear that you are learning the piano. Do you like it?

Fred was not in any of the photos which I sent you but he is on some which we took here, and if they are finished I shall send them with this letter. I am very busy packing this morning and this afternoon I am going to ask all the gentlemen to come and sit on my boxes because they won't shut.

This afternoon I have to make a net for our camp beds, because beside the mosquitos in the Ucayali River there are tiny little black flies which sting even worse and they get through the net which we have. We have seen several lovely butterflies, but we shall not start collecting until we get to Orton.

Collecting was a favourite pastime of Victorian travellers. It was perhaps done rather indiscriminately, but then almost everything was new.

The letters sent to Lizzie which she mentions below were never brought home, so it is not known how George hurt his arm. He was an engineer, so it may have been an accident at work.

German Consulate, Iquitos, Peru
26 April 1897

Mr dear Dad and Mama,

I received two letters from you last Friday, two days after my birthday, also one from Nellie and one from Rosie. I was so delighted I have read them all at least six times over. It was the first news we had had for 3 months and the last we shall get for another 3 months. They were dated February, one on the 7th and one on the 28th.

I was pleased to hear that you were all well and everything going on all right. I hope that Bib likes her situation, it will be much nicer for her when the fine weather comes. We have forgotten all about frost and snow, we are having such very hot weather all the time. I hope George's arm is better now. You must give my love to the Straker family, as soon as we are settled in Orton I shall write to them, but I am so pleased that they like my Polly and she is happy with them.

I am sure when we get to Orton I shall have a whole pile of letters. I am looking forward to them already. You don't know how I long for news from you all; no one can know it until they have been away for a few months.

On your birthday we were steaming up the Amazon on board the *Rio Branco*, but we thought of you. I did not think you were 57 years old, you seem much younger to me. I do not think you will ever get old, the children won't let you.

Rosie seems to be happy in her new home. I only hope Ben will prosper in his new business.

I think you can safely send off the magazines now, I shall be so glad of something from the old world to read. I have nearly finished all my books.

We hope to be in Orton, three months from now. I have seen a picture of our future house, it is very large with a verandah running all round. We shall have it to ourselves except when Mr Vaca Diez is in Orton, then he will live there too. The servants are Indians and can only be made to work by the whip. To be kind is no good, they only laugh at you. They are lazy people, but I think they are faithful. The climate makes everyone lazy, I cannot work at all, I stare out of the window, sleep and eat, but work I cannot.

Lizzie sat patiently in the Weisses' house in Iquitos, putting on weight though never mentioning her diet. An Amazon menu seldom reaches gourmet class and it is unlikely that she went to any of the small eating-houses – even less so to the taverns – run mostly by Italians and Spaniards. The German kitchen received tinned food from Europe, including fine *petits pois* from France. Milk and eggs were scarce, and the daily fare consisted of dried or 'jerked' meat, dried cod or *bacalão* from the Brazilian coast, and fresh *paiche* – the arapaima, one of the largest fish in the Amazon, some of which weigh 300 lb and measure more than nine feet long. Add to this unusual fare potatoes, which had to be imported and were usually inedible on arrival, and the main course of a meal could well be unsensational. Luckily, champagne was plentiful.

So when, at the end of April, Vaca Diez was ready to leave, Lizzie was too. She did not face the next stage of the journey with open apprehension or excitement, but with just a slight lift to her spirits. They had the *Laura* on their terms, too.

We are leaving Iquitos on Wednesday by the steam launch *Laura*; she has two decks, on the upper one we shall be six people, on the lower about 20. We are also sending up 2 smaller launches with about 12 people, so out of the 500 we are 40 left, but we are not sorry, it would have been difficult to get them all up by this route. As it is we are leaving nearly all of our cargo here, in charge of some 6 people, and shall send down for it later on. They have kindly taken pity on me and made me a screen of tarpaulin and also a WC. Before the launch had no WC, the people had to sit on the rails. She also has no cabin, but I shall be alright with my screen. I also have a French maid, the wife of our cook, to wait on me during the journey. I am a swell, you don't know what a fuss they make of me.

The Amazon was just below its highest level. Leaving the Weisses' house, with Indian porters carrying the last-minute baggage, Lizzie and Fred set out along the crumbling pavement of Prospero Street; they had to step between piles of debris, dirt and human excreta, and Lizzie clasped a perfumed handkerchief to her nose. Apart from Mr Weiss' house, only the gaol and the Prefectura, the local seat of government, looked fit to last.

Getting down to the river involved scrambling over logs littered with rat-infested garbage: for convenience in those days – not so much through pressure of space – some people lived in houses built on rafts, which settled on the mud in the dry season but flooded when the river was high. Some of this she mentioned to her parents, leaving them to supply any further details from their own imagination.

We are having such an experience you have no idea, passing through beautiful country and seeing all sorts of people. Some of the Indians live entirely on the rafts by the banks of the river and are almost animals in their habits.

I had a nice birthday, they all drank my health in champagne. I had some nice presents, too, a pretty ring from Fred, a box of Paris scent and soap from Vaca Diez and a pair of flower vases from a gentleman of our expedition, also several bouquets from the gentlemen here. I only wanted news from home.

All the way from Pará they had travelled almost due west up the Amazon. With very little variation in width and even less in vegetation, the Amazon cuts across South America just below the Equator, through the world's most extensive rain forest. At Iquitos, four miles separate one tree-lined bank from the other, and only an island in midstream opposite the Malecón lessens the impact of the river's true size. Ocean-going cargo ships visit Iquitos infrequently now, and few ever go further upstream. But in 1897 the economics of the upper Amazon were different, vessels were smaller, and above Iquitos the Peruvian Amazon tributaries alone reach more than a quarter of a million square miles of land. In the high-water season, from December to May, a further 5500 miles of river are navigable to ships with a draught of up to eight feet, and another 4000 miles for steamers drawing up to four feet. Iron steamships of all kinds were a familiar sight. Lanchas, twin- and three-deck steamers and the occasional Mississippi-style stern-wheeler were busily plying the river routes.

Upstream from Iquitos the Amazon continues for almost 150 miles, gradually curving southwest until the name Amazon is dropped in favour of the two immense tributaries, the Marañon and the Ucayali, pouring in from the Andes. Each has its band of supporters claiming that one or the other leads to the true source of the Amazon. On the right, looking upstream, the Marañon, the heavyweight in volume, begins life at over 16,000 feet, and hardly any distance as the crow flies from Lima, the capital. On the left the Ucayali, with less water, but longer, starts much farther south in the Andes, as Lizzie was to find out. Upstream along both these giants other rivers can be followed well into the mountains, where a break in the clouds may give a glimpse of snow.

Fitzcarrald had a *barraca* alongside the Urubamba River, a tributary of the Ucayali, at Mishagua, some weeks' journey away to the south. Before leaving Lizzie wrote home, without mentioning Fitzcarrald by name.

Our next stopping place will be Mishagua after 4 weeks up the Ucayali River. It is a town consisting of one hut and the huts of the Indians. We have an introduction to the one hut, so we shall be looked after. We expect to stay there two weeks, and then begins our canoe journey. The water is too low for the launches to come any higher, that will be the most difficult part of our little trip, but we shall manage alright. Vaca Diez likes to take care of himself and we are always with him. We are taking plenty of nice wine and brandy with us and also biscuits. We shall get no bread after we leave here.

. . . If I get a chance I will write more from Mishagua, that is the last place from which we can write until we reach Orton. Give my love to everybody and tell them not to get tired of writing.

Now goodbye my dear Dad, Mama, as soon as I am settled I shall write to all the boys and girls in turn so as to keep their memories awake.

With love from your loving daughter,

Lizzie

Fred sends his love to you all, he is very busy at present.

They must have gone directly into the Ucayali before stopping at one of the many small settlements there. Once in the Ucayali the only change is in the current, which is usually faster, about three and a half knots. Strong eddies and swirling water turn navigation into a permanent headache at the best of times, but the falling water level in May makes for slow progress. In due course they reached Contamana, a rubber gatherers' outpost on the left bank.

On board *Laura*, Contamana, Peru
Saturday, 15 May 1897

My dear Dad and Mama,

We have been on our way now exactly a fortnight and are about a quarter of the journey to Mishagua. The water is very low and sometimes we have nearly run ashore but it has rained very heavily so perhaps it will rise again.

We are getting along very slowly, we travel for two days and then have to wait two days for our smaller launches which cannot keep up with us.

We are very comfortable on this launch. I have a lovely little cabin and plenty of people to wait on us and this so far has been the nicest part of the journey. Fred has a lot to worry him though, everything he has to arrange and settle. People who are not satisfied come to him with their troubles.

The river is most beautiful. It is even grander than the Amazon, though it is full of small whirlpools and the current is enormous, sometimes going with full speed we do not advance a yard for half an hour.

Fred and the doctor have shot plenty of alligators, this river is full of them. They also shot a wild pig and some garcias, those are the birds which have the nice feathers on the breast.

We have stopped at several villages and at all of them I come in for presents. The people are very hospitable, they send me fowls, eggs, bananas, flowers and at one place they sent me a bundle of maize, all sorts of queer presents. They think I am a somebody in this country.

The garcia of which she spoke was a species of egret, whose feathers were imported into Europe at this time, in particular for decorating hats. If Lizzie had been on the Marañon, with its shorter route to the Andes via Yurimaguas, she would not have been considered such an unusual sight, but on the Ucayali beyond Contamana she was one of only a few European travellers. The development of the rubber trade had ensured exploration, and most of the large tributaries entering from the Andes on the right bank were well-used routes to the mountains. One, the Pichis River, led to the hazardous Pichis Trail, open even now; though as a result of neglect its long, zigzag path has degenerated into a nightmarish scramble through forested ravines.

Along the lower Ucayali Lizzie met the Shipibo and Conibo Indians, the first forest people whom she saw on her journey. Modesty may have prevented her staring too hard at their painted body decorations, for the

Indians were only partly clothed. Women of the tribe would have worn nothing more than a simple skirt or loincloth, and some of the men may have been completely naked – 'very strange in their dress and habits,' she said euphemistically. The Shipibos, the tiny 'monkey people', and the Conibos, the 'fish people', tended to fight each other. Both blackened their teeth by chewing a specially grown pepper, and some may even have filed their teeth, but despite their appearance they were friendly to Lizzie. These small people have been a source of fascination to anthropologists for many years. In Lizzie's day they covered their bodies with curious geometric designs of finely drawn lines, using similar patterns on their pottery and canoe paddles. Among their customs, travellers had noted ritual female defloration and the practice of deforming their babies' heads.

Lizzie wrote home about the country through which they were now travelling, which had produced the latest member of her ever-changing menagerie of pets.

I also have had a dear little monkey given to me, it is so tame and runs about all day catching flies and spiders. When it is tired it comes to be nursed and curls itself up under my arm or in my neck. It talks to me in its own language and I always know what it wants.

At one of the places I went ashore and did some revolver shooting. I did not shoot anybody or anything that I wanted to.

The Indians are quite friendly up this river but they are very savage in their dress and habits. I would not like to meet them alone. Most of them are very shy.

In some of the places there are thousands of mosquitos, they make you so hot and irritable, the only way to keep them off is to keep fanning yourself. In other places we have none at all and when the ship is going we don't feel them.

All the villages are in the same style, only huts made with palm leaves, bamboo sticks and rough wood with little or no furniture, all the people sleep in hammocks.

I do not know if you will get this letter. We are leaving them here and the next steamer down will take them to Iquitos, but I shall write by every chance I get, to let you know how we are getting along.

We are both well. I have never felt so well in my life. Fred has grown a beard and looks quite fatherly.

Sometimes the weather is very cool and one night I actually shivered; but at present it is very hot, it rains almost every day.

I hope you are all well and everything going on in the same way.

You must tell Rosie and Alice this little news as I shall not write to them. We have been away five months today, it does not seem long to me, does it to you?

Alice was the eldest of the Mathys children, respected by her younger siblings because she had had the task of keeping them in order. Lizzie seldom talked of her – she had married before Lizzie and was living in Southampton.

We do not know when we shall arrive in Orton. I shall be very glad, I am tired of travelling. You get so dirty and your clothes get dirty and dressing is so uncomfortable, it will be so nice to be able to dress and stretch myself in a room again. We live very well and have queer dishes sometimes. We have cooked bananas and *euchre* with every meal and also maize roasted, which is very nice. I always enjoy my food because I get so hungry. Now goodbye, with love to everybody and to yourselves from your loving daughter.

. . . I do not think you will find this village on the map, it is very small, but the next one, Cumaria, you might. We shall be there in two days.

Names or the importance of the places along the route have changed since Lizzie's journey. Pucallpa, a busy river port on the Ucayali, did not exist in the 1890s, and has grown since the road link was built across the Andes to Lima. The village of Yarina, five miles from Pucallpa, on Yarina-Cocha, a lagoon whose name means Lake of Yarina (a palm producing vegetable ivory), was on nineteenth-century maps but the *Laura* did not stop there. Instead they continued upriver, expecting to reach Cumaria. The famous House of Cumaria, built in the rubber days, still stands well back from the river on the left bank, and at one time was the best place to stay. Ask a river man and he would count the distance in days to and from Cumaria.

They kept going, for the only way they could complete the journey was by spending long hours on the river. Sometimes they kept close to the forest when navigating an inside bend, and then they would head away across the river following the deep channel of a meander. By mid-June they had reached another major junction. On the right, coming from behind a high bank, the River Tambo, which rises in the mountains in the far south of Peru, enters the Ucayali. The Tambo changes name three times as it tumbles towards the Amazon lowlands. Apurimac, the 'great speaker', is the name used by the highland Incas; among the forest tribes it becomes the Ene, and then the Tambo. Lizzie had arrived at the place where the Tambo is joined by another powerful river, the Urubamba, which rises beyond Cuzco, the ancient

Inca capital. Up there in the mountains the river is called the Vilcanota, though by the time it passes Machu Picchu, the 'lost' Inca city, it has become the Urubamba. The point where the Tambo and Urubamba meet is isolated even now, and the only quick way in is by light aircraft. When Lizzie stopped there it was a wilderness known only to a few *caucheros*.

In this part of the Amazon the forest Indian was the traditional labourer and the *patrónes* organised Indian hunts or *correrías*. The tribes would be rounded up, the strongest members taken away and the weaklings tortured and killed. One American traveller in the late 1940s found a 'torture box' or 'punishment coffin' still being used by a *patrón* close to the place where Lizzie wrote her next letter. The box, made of wood and corrugated metal, was little more than body size, and once inside the unfortunate victim had no room to move and was left to roast in the sun. Often the prisoner went mad – according to the American, screaming for mercy. Some have said it was an exaggeration, and hopefully it was, but fifteen years later Indians, including children, were still being kept in serfdom at the same place.

On board the *Laura*, Tambo River, Peru

16 June 1897

My dear Dad and Mama,

What do you think of my address to begin with. We have reached so far and here we have stuck. We are just at the point where the Ucayali, the Urubamba and the Tambo River join, within a week from Mishagua. The water is too low for us to get any higher; we tried but ran ashore and had great difficulty in getting off again, but we did and have anchored just a little way up the Tambo River in a very lovely spot, quite wild. No one has been here before. We have a very nice spring coming from the mountains which we appreciate very much, fresh water is quite a luxury for us now. The mountains are on one side, simply grand, they make the air so cool. It is a most lovely climate.

We have cleared a space in the forest and every afternoon we go to sleep there in our hammocks and at 4 o'clock our dinner is brought up to us there. It would be more enjoyable if there were not so many insects though; the wood is swarming with large ants and beetles, and we have a nice little collection of spiders. Tremendous centipedes and snakes have intruded into our garden. Now I must tell you our plans, but there is so much to tell you that I don't know where to begin.

Fitzcarrald's *barraca* was far up the Urubamba. Above the Tambo confluence the Urubamba remains broad and in many ways similar to the Ucayali for at least a couple of days' travel. But thereafter the dangers increase. The river becomes shallower and contains many hidden obstructions, mostly dead trees and sandbanks. During the rainy season the powerful current rips at the banks, undermining forest and toppling many yards of it into the river. Hundreds of thousands of tons of earth and wood can collapse with a roar heard miles away; suddenly the river is filled with mud and debris. Yet nothing stops the relentless pressure of water pouring down these Andean rivers. Trees 150 feet high, with splayed buttress roots up to 50 feet across, are hurled along as wood chips in a wind. At sharp bends where whirlpools form these leviathans are spun as easily as a child's top, their leaves and smaller branches stripped away in the torrent. Then, as the water level drops, the trees get stuck. A rhythmically bobbing twig stationary in the fast current is a sure sign of a snag below. Sometimes there is not even a twig – just a curling ripple on the surface.

We tried, four of us, to get up the Urubamba in one of the small launches. We were out two hours; during that time we ran ashore eleven times, then drifted back with the current within sight of the *Laura* when we struck a tree which was under the water. We nearly capsized but with the exception of one man overboard whom we rescued, and the loss of our pots and pans, no damage was done. We frightened the people on the *Laura*, they could see us and screamed and shouted, they thought we were lost. We all had had enough by that time, so came back. The next day we sent a large canoe with half a dozen people to Mishagua. They are to bring back canoes for us all, so we shall have to finish the remainder of our journey in canoes. We expect them tomorrow.

One of our launches has not turned up yet, but we had news of her today. All her crew deserted so we sent them help. You have no idea of the strength of these rivers, it is impossible to swim against the current and sometimes the ship goes back instead of advancing. We passed over a cataract and through the 'Devil's Whirlpool' quite safely. We all had to hold on tight and felt a bit nervous; now the worst part of the river is over.

But they had left Iquitos too late. Vaca Diez may have misjudged the river, though his boatmen would have warned him. Lizzie seemed to enjoy the danger and uncertainty, and at last there was a delay during which she could spend time in the forest, exploring and looking for animals which she described in her next letter home. Tigers, of course, are not found in South America, but the early explorers used the name *tigre* for the jaguar. As Lizzie noted, these animals, the largest South American carnivores, are powerful swimmers. The anteater with the long nose was an unusual encounter; giant anteaters are not common, and her observation probably meant that they had camped on relatively high ground. By 'wild pig' Lizzie meant the sharp-tusked peccary; one of the species, the white-lipped peccary, which forages in large troops, is said to be more dangerous as a collective force than a single jaguar. The meat is good, as Lizzie said, particularly so in the way she tried it with a salad of palm hearts. Vaca Diez' special wine may have been an imported luxury, but it is more likely that he had introduced Lizzie to a mixture of *aguardiente* and fruit juice, perhaps adding wild herbs. 'A tonic, highly recommended – Señora,' he would have said as subtle introduction.

Since we left Cumaria we have only met with Indians. They have all been friendly though you have to treat them like children and they will do anything for a bottle of spirit. I gave some of the women some of those mixed biscuits with sweets on and some small mirrors which were packed with the butter as advertisements; they were delighted and very much amused with the glasses. They are very savage both in their dress and manners.

I have been exploring round the borders of the forest and followed up a tiger's footprints, but he had evidently crossed the river; we traced him there. We also came across several alligators' footprints, but we did not meet with any animals. We had an anteater close by, one of those with the long noses. We shoot the wild pigs and eat them; it is the only fresh meat we get except turtles. The pork is a trifle strong but otherwise good; eaten with a salad made from the palm tree it is not bad. We have no more bread and no wine except a special kind which I and Vaca Diez drink. We shall also run out of coffee this week.

We send out men hunting and fishing to keep up our store. We have eaten stork steaks and wild duck and snipe. We have not got to monkeys yet, though some of our people shot and ate some. My little monkey I have lost; I was very sorry, he was very affectionate, but we have the little puppy to take his place, which was given to us at one of the villages; the two large dogs are my friends now that they know me, they feel the heat though, poor things. Everyone keeps well I am glad to say. I had headache from the mountain air here I think but I am used to it now and am quite well. I have taken to the dress of the country, given up corsets altogether and wear blouses with elastic through the hem at the bottom, like boys' sailor blouses at the waist. It is so comfortable and free. I shall be quite an athlete when I return. I have to climb and jump in our walks.

Now I wonder how you all are at home. Of course we have not heard from you since we left Iquitos. We cannot get letters until we reach Orton and this will be the last time I can write to you until then. We hope to be in Orton six weeks or more from now. Our launches we shall leave somewhere until the water rises in November. I am looking forward to the budget [a leather pouch used for sending letters] I shall receive when we get there.

Fancy, this is June and last news was dated February. Six months yesterday we left London; half of one year gone already. I hope they will all pass as quickly. We talk about our journey home even now. I would not like to live in this country always, though I am enjoying the trip immensely, it is such an experience and one I always longed for.

I have to keep on wondering what you are all doing, it will be so nice when we can keep up our correspondence regularly; once a month we shall have a mail both in and out, so they will have to be very long letters. I have finished all the books I brought with me, so will you send me all the magazines you don't want.

Butterflies and birds make this part of the Amazon a naturalist's paradise. Since it is close to the mountains the rainfall and climate are varied, giving almost a spring and summer change. Then, as the river level falls, many thousands of a single species of butterfly gather at one time on the exposed mud.

Fred is collecting butterflies. He has thirty already, some beauties amongst them too. He has a nice pointed beard now and looks so well; he sends his love to everybody. He is too lazy to write, I do all that.

Give my love to all at home and all friends and tell everybody not to get tired of writing. I wish we could come and stay a week with you. With best love to you dear Dad and Mum from your loving daughter,

Lizzie

The canoes have come but not the missing launch.

Chapter Five

'The Indians called me always Mama'

Six months after leaving Pará Lizzie and Fred arrived in Mishagua, home of the pioneer *cauchero* Fitzcarrald, from where he commanded a network of rivers among the foothills of the Andes. In the last stage of their journey Lizzie and Fred travelled by canoe up the Urubamba. In this section the river can be 300 yards wide and rushing downhill towards the Amazon quite beyond control. Here, where the rocky feet of the Andes bar the river's escape, cliffs rise sheer from the water's edge, breaking the flow into treacherous currents. Many species of birds choose these places to breed, and beautifully woven oropendolas' nests hang above the torrent like well-filled Christmas stockings. Parakeets in screeching flocks burst from the trees, and the occasional *maquisapa* or black spider monkey swings lazily through the forest canopy. Lizzie now seemed really to be entering the spirit of the venture, and her view of the Indians, whom she had previously considered as savages, in line with general attitudes, was changing with experience.

> The canoe journey I enjoyed immensely. We had two fine Indians, noblemen they were and very proud. To see them walk was a treat and strength enormous. They used to get out into the water quite naked and pull our heavy canoe over the waterfalls, sometimes four in one day we passed. The English Doctor and one Peruvian gent travelled with us. We used to start at 7 in the morning, travel until 10 o'clock, when we stopped for breakfast. The Indians made the fire and we cooked. Then we all bathed in the river, I also . . . .

It was the custom for men and women to bathe together, though Woodroffe said that the women in Iquitos kept to one part of the river. Lizzie continues:

> [We] went on again until ½ past 4 when we pulled up for the night. The Indians made fire again, which they kept up all night to keep away the animals. They used to make us palm leaf huts to sleep in also. We used to have our dinner and go to bed. Nearly every night we used to hear tigers and other animals close by, and once I lay awake and heard one about six yards off from our tent, but they never disturbed us. As a rule they do not attack unless

wounded, or if you have a dog with you they make straight for it; they are very fond of them [dogs]. But I used to feel a bit nervous all the same.

On the way up here the Indians and gents used to give everything which they shoot and catch to you. The Indians called me always Mama. Fish they shoot with bow and arrow and we had some fine ones. We also had monkeys, parrots and various other birds which we were only too glad to eat, for you get awfully tired of tinned meats.

Baron Justus von Liebig's famous extract of meat was already being produced in Uruguay, and had become a favourite addition to the traveller's hamper. Obviously it could become too much of a good thing.

. . . then we had bananas and rice. It is fine to watch the Indians hunt. They creep along without a sound. The names of ours were Sebastian and Maritius. They wore long robes until we gave them a shirt and trousers each. They are very fond of dress and every morning used to look at themselves in my glass. They always cooked their own meals and made some queer dishes. They used to give us some. You must not refuse to eat with them or they think you do not trust them.

I think I have told you most of our news and hope you will receive this letter. We think we shall be here for three weeks and in Orton six or eight weeks from now. If only Bert could have been with us, how he would have enjoyed our adventures. We did not meet a soul during the whole journey. The Indians keep to the interior in these parts.

Sebastian and Maritius, their Campa Indian boatmen, worked hard keeping to the side of the river, using powerful eddies and backcurrents to ease the way upstream. At places where broad shingle banks form on bends, the boatmen crossed the river in order to use deeper, slow-flowing channels.

Remote though it is, this part of the Urubamba has been used as a route from Inca times, possibly even earlier. And soon after the Spanish conquest of the Inca Empire, missionary priests ventured from the mountains to the forests of the Urubamba and Ucayali. A mission post was set up on a tributary of the Urubamba in 1805, and its Franciscan inhabitants tried hard to contact the Indians downriver. Sebastian and Maritius are not true Indian names, so they must have had some contact with outsiders. The 'long robes' which Lizzie mentions were *cushmas*, made of native cotton and resembling a long poncho; a tightly woven *cushma* is an excellent blanket against the cool air of those Andean foothills.

I am sure I am not born to be drowned, for we have been near it many times, but our Indians managed the canoe splendidly. They stopped always at the very second and seemed to enjoy the danger. I must say that I did too. You get sort of excited and then don't feel afraid. If we wanted to reach a certain spot on the other side of the river we had to get a mile beyond it before we attempted to cross, then everyone paddles for their very lives (I also) and the current takes you back to the spot you want. Then the Indians catch a tree or hold on to the shore with their sticks, then you can go on again. Fancy going down river the rate of 12 miles an hour amidst rushing waters when you are paddling your hardest to get up, and if you strike a tree or rock under the water you are done for. The Urubamba is one of the most beautiful and grand rivers you can imagine, high rocks, with forest growing to the very edge and springs coming down from them. There must be any amount of gold. Then there are the beautiful birds and butterflies, storks, parrots, pigeons, toucans and any amount of bright coloured small birds, troops of monkeys swinging amongst the trees; it is grand. The rest of our trip is not dangerous especially if we meet the launch. Some Indians are going down to Cumaria and will take this letter. When you will get it I do not know, but I hope it will be soon, for you must always be wondering where we were. We are both in splendid health and hope you are all also, perhaps you will see us sooner than expected. Now, goodbye, dear Dad and Mama and love to everybody.

Lizzie and Fred were welcomed at Mishagua by Fitzcarrald. His large house, built on low stilts, was fronted by a wide verandah of split *chonta* palm laid in strips. This tough wood – its own hardness renders it useful as nails – also makes a convenient, self-cleaning floor: not only is it durable, but small pieces of rubbish and dirt fall through the cracks to the ground below.

Carlos Fermín Fitzcarrald was only twenty-six when he reached Iquitos from Lima, the Peruvian capital. One of a family of seven, Fitzcarrald had been born in the chill mountain town of San Luis de Huari, where he first went to school. Later he was sent to Lima, and embarked on a stormy career at the Liceo Peruano; after one brawl he was left for dead. Though he recovered quickly, his name was then blackened by rumours that he had spied for Chile. Chile and Peru were warring over valuable territory containing saltpetre deposits, used in

Above *The Napo River, a major tributary of the Amazon, was passed by Lizzie on her way to Iquitos. It was down this river that the first-ever recorded full-length descent of the Amazon was begun by Francisco de Orellana in 1542*

Previous page *Lizzie sent postcards from Paris, and toucan feathers which she posted with a letter from Orton*

Right *Dr Antonio Vaca Diez, Bolivian physician, scholar and explorer. He* developed a huge business in the heart of the Bolivian rubber forests within a few years of the first exploration there

Far right *Don Nicholás Suárez, Bolivian master businessman, Amazon pioneer and great hero of his country for his defence of its frontiers. Suárez, who owned property in London, was known as the Rockefeller of rubber*

Above *At the height of the annual flood in late February, the Amazon near Iquitos spreads out, covering thousands of square miles. When the Rio Branco steamed upriver in this season, it collected supplies from settlements like these*

Right *As people moved along the Amazon waterways, colonising the* rubber forests, they built simple houses. All the materials came from the forest and the only imports were Winchester carbines, clothes, food and alcohol

Far right *The huts of Machiguenga Indians in a small rain-forest clearing are surrounded by their 'gardens' where they grow yuca – sweet manioc – sugar and cacao*

Above *The Manú River in the Peruvian Amazon is bordered by some of the most inaccessible forests in all the Amazon*

Above right *Riverboats from the turn of the century have mostly disappeared from the Amazon. These were collected and restored by the German film director Werner Herzog for his production* Fitzcarraldo, *based on the life of the Peruvian* cauchero *Carlos Fermín Fitzcarrald, whose untimely death was recorded by Lizzie*

Right *One relic of the rubber days, the Fitzcarrald, sits high and dry in the forests of the Madre de Dios. At one time the river ran nearby, but over the years its course has changed and the boat is now beached a mile inland*

Above A carretón or wooden-
wheeled cart drawn by oxen is floated
across a tributary of the Beni on
a ranch belonging to the Suárez family

Left Fitzcarrald founded his business
house at the confluence of the Rivers
Mishagua (left and brown) and
Urubamba (right and clear), some
3000 miles upriver from Pará

manufacturing fertilisers. So Fitzcarrald chose a profitable, self-imposed exile in the Amazon, hiding at times under the alias of 'Carlos Fernando'. From the point of view of seclusion, Mishagua could not have been better. Upstream, the Urubamba is treacherous, blocked by the Pongo de Mainique, the most dangerous rapids in Peru. Downstream, Iquitos was weeks away, and outside the front door the River Mishagua led to unexplored forests.

Bit by bit Fitzcarrald built up his power as a *cauchero*. The rubber all around Mishagua was his for the taking, and by employing Campa and Piro Indians on the best terms he could offer – gifts and *aguardiente*, which they never refused – Fitzcarrald gained both their support and protection. He sent rubber down to Iquitos where he had a partner, and except for infrequent visits to that town he stayed in his retreat, where he had a well-fortified house surrounded by small fields and planted with many flowers, some grown from seeds imported from Europe; traces of it remain even now. Fitzcarrald married Aurora Velasco before his Mishagua days, and their children were later educated in Paris; in one of her letters Lizzie mentioned 'the Frenchman who was manager'. Fitzcarrald had established European connections.

Isolation and being first on the spot gave Fitzcarrald leverage to deal with businessmen of the calibre of Suárez and Vaca Diez. The new route was an asset, and he held all the cards. From the air the land between these rivers seems impassable, with dense forest for 1500 miles in every direction except west, where the Andes rise. A spur of the mountains, its outline often softened by cloud, descends to the Amazon. Among the low ridges of this far-off hill the Mishagua River begins on one side and the Caspajali River on the other. Water from the Caspajali ends up in the Beni and eventually flows to the Madeira. In the deep jungle covering the top of the ridge, some of the least-explored country in all the Amazon, just a few steps separate two river systems. But the Mishagua has tributaries and so does the Caspajali, and other rivers also begin at the divide; Fitzcarrald was faced by a multi-dimensional puzzle.

He soon learnt of passes linking the rivers: Campas and Piros knew from hunting expeditions how a network of streams was hidden in the forest, some streams going one way and others in the opposite direction. Fitzcarrald began to explore, but it was not easy. The principal danger came from Indian tribes who were neither Piro nor Campa: deeper within the forest lived tribes speaking an unrelated language and, as Fitzcarrald discovered, these Indians always attacked his Piro guides.

In his earliest explorations Fitzcarrald was hoping to find the headwaters of the Purus, a major river which runs almost parallel to the

Madeira and into the Amazon. After months of walking, wading, clambering through rapids but always somehow miraculously avoiding mishap, Fitzcarrald located not just one crossing but three or four. Had he reached the Purus? At first he was not sure, but in August 1893 he crossed the divide and, after following a small stream, found himself on the way to the broad, island-studded Peruvian river called Madre de Dios or Mother of God, a tributary of the Beni. A year later he was back at the Madre de Dios again, this time reaching a *barraca* under the control of Suárez, who was at that time pushing well into Peru.

Then came Fitzcarrald's decisive move, one he knew he had to make to hold off the Bolivian advance. He steamed in with a small launch, the *Contamana*, bought on credit in Iquitos. Well upriver the three-ton boat was taken apart so that mules and porters could portage it over the divide; on the other side it was reassembled. Fitzcarrald thus became master of two rivers, a stratagem that paid off in his first deal with Suárez.

Fitzcarrald made that epic crossing in July 1896, just a year before Fred and Lizzie arrived in Mishagua. Rubber was already moving out of Bolivia across the divide by then, and goods carried from Iquitos cost less in the Beni than those carried up the Madeira. Despite the length of the route, it was a tempting alternative to the Madeira, particularly when the high water between November and May allowed navigation by large steam launches. That left just the problem of transhipment at the divide. Piro porters were no problem for Fitzcarrald, but Suárez suggested a more modern alternative – a short narrow-gauge railway.

Fred and Lizzie arrived at Mishagua just as business began to look good for Fitzcarrald. Vaca Diez would be the next to agree terms. The entire region, including the Orton with its London backing, was about to begin a phase of rapid development.

Urubamba, Mishagua, Peru
20 July 1897

My dear Dad, Mama and everybody,

I am pleased to be able to write that we arrived here safely two weeks ago, after a ten days trip in a canoe up the most dreadful river you can imagine. It is all waterfalls, whirlpools, strong currents, rocks and trees. Vaca Diez asked us to go in the launch, *Adolfito*, with him, but everyone advised us to go in a canoe and there is no safer way of travelling in these rivers.

Lizzie then described a tragedy that changed the whole balance of power in the upper Amazon.

We now thank Heaven that we chose the canoe, for three days

down from Mishagua the chain of the *Adolfito* broke and the current took her and she went down, and the most dreadful thing of all, Vaca Diez was drowned together with the gentleman who owns this place. He went down to meet Vaca Diez and joined him in the launch. Also one engineer and the steward were drowned; five others who could swim saved themselves just by the skin of their teeth and were brought along by the other canoes which were behind. Poor Mrs Fitzcarrald has four children, she is, of course, dreadfully upset. She thinks it is through us that she has lost her husband. He received us most kindly when we arrived here and gave us a room in his house, the only house here; the others are all Indians and of course have their huts. The day after, he made up his mind to go down and fetch Vaca Diez because he did not trust the launch, so he had two canoes prepared and everything that he thought would make the journey more comfortable for Vaca Diez. Evidently he was persuaded to stop on the launch. It is a most dreadful thing and we can't help feeling more for him than the others.

Lizzie's account appears to be the only near-eyewitness record of the disaster, which occurred at a treacherous spot known as Sepa, now the site of a jungle prison colony. But although in the 1890s Sepa was seen as a *mal paso*, a bad place to pass, was the water that bad in July? Could the accident have been deliberately planned? Convenient 'accidents' were a business tool of the rubber boom and Sepa is not the worst place on the river. The circumstances still leave a question mark today.

This has been a most unfortunate expedition. Out of the 500 we are 16 left, Vaca Diez the director for Bolivia dead, and Suárez, one of the London directors, died whilst we were in Pará. We do not know now if the Company will exist, but we are all going on to Orton and shall wait for instructions there. It may be that we shall have to return to Europe. Fred went down with some others to search for the bodies. They found Mr Fitzcarrald washed up on some trees, some days down. They buried him in the forest. Fred then returned and sent one canoe down to the Tambo to fetch some cargo and two gents who were left there; also to continue the search. Some of the luggage was saved, but we have had to leave it on a sandbank at present, we can get no men and no canoes and we can only wait for someone to arrive and take charge of this business here; also to give us some Indians and canoes to continue our journey. There are two tribes of Indians here, the Piros and the Campas; they are friendly to us.

When they heard their master, or *patrón* as they called him, was dead, they threatened to kill the manager (a Frenchman), they all hate him because he illtreats them. So we had to keep watch during the night, all the gents around, and next day we sent him off in a canoe down to Iquitos. Since then they have been quiet enough. Some of them want Fred to be their *patrón* and to take them to Bolivia with him; when they have no master they are lost because they are half-civilised already. Fred humours them at present, of course, we have to keep friendly with them, but I do not know if they will come with us. The gents take it in turns to keep watch during the night and have always rifles and revolvers handy in case of an attack. They sleep on the balcony and all us women in two rooms which are locked. I can tell you, I have had enough of travelling in these uncivilised parts during these seven months, we have had the experience of a lifetime.

So Fred was in charge of the remnants of the party, stuck over 3000 miles up the Amazon and comprising, at Lizzie's last estimate, an English doctor, one Peruvian 'gentleman', five survivors from the *Adolfito*, Mrs Fitzcarrald, £10 and several dogs. Lizzie needed no intuition to realise that Fitzcarrald's death was a turning point.

He was going to supply us with canoes and Indians for the rest of our journey; now we shall have to wait until another partner arrives and who is now in Iquitos. We sent the news down to be telegraphed to London, also that we were safe, which I hope you heard, because up till then we had always been with Vaca Diez and people would think that we were drowned also. We have made up our minds to go to Orton and send up the news there, and to send down a launch with provisions to meet us in the Madre de Dios.

Mishagua turned out to involve another long wait, so Lizzie had time for three more letters. Among her observations in this corner of the Amazon she noted the earth-eating of the children, a habit best known among the tribes of the Purus River. It was a subject that fascinated the Victorians, and many travellers' accounts recorded it. Orton, published three years after Lizzie was born, said: 'Women, as they lie in bed sleepless and restless, will pull out pieces of mud from the adjoining walls of their room to gratify their strange appetite, or will soothe a squalling brat by tempting it with a lump of the same material.' The most plausible modern explanations of what anthropologists term 'geophagy' range from an exaggeration to a ritual contact with the earth, or a way of getting salt in an otherwise saltless diet.

Lizzie talks of other rivers, tiny streams such as the Mansi or the winding Manú on the other side of the divide. And as usual when she had spare time she reflected on her own pets and other people's children. The 'piwns' which irritated her so much are piums, which live only in sunlight, so they can be avoided by retreating into the darkness of a hut. Usually, though, by that time the damage has already been done – hundreds of tiny bites which, according to a person's sensitivity, may produce massive bumps; even a mild reaction leaves painfully itching spots.

Mishagua, Peru
18 August 1897

My dear Dad, Mama and everybody,

We are still waiting here for someone to come up from Iquitos, but as the river has fallen considerably it takes a long time to come up river.

Some rubber cutters have arrived from the Mansi River and one of them is going down to Iquitos and will take letters for us, so I thought I would just let you know that we are safe and well. They also expect 50 rubber cutters to arrive during the week, so it will be a bit livelier here.

With the exception of an attack of dysentry, I am very well and Fred also. Dysentry is very common here on account of the bad food and the only way to cure it is to starve yourself, which I did for a week. The consequence was I was very weak and homesick, but now I am alright again. The food is very bad, this week we have lived on dried monkey and dried birds, which the people brought with them, then we have rice and bananas. There is hardly any nourishment in the food at all. I take condensed milk during the day, I get so hungry. They are expecting some tinned meats up this week from Iquitos, so we shall have a little bit of a change.

Two Indians have died from dysentry, but the only cure they use for every illness is cold water, so nine cases out of ten they kill their patients. When anyone dies all the women start weeping and wailing and making an awful noise and the next day everybody gets drunk. One boy died here through eating dirt, which a lot of them do in this part of the country. You cannot stop them when they begin, but they always die. Fred has also sent down to Cumaria for provisions for our next journey; our people have such enormous appetites that we are running short, you should see the platefuls of rice they eat. They all look to Fred now that Dr Vaca Diez is dead, so he has a lot to think about and is a little bit worried. He only has about £10 left of the expedition money, all the other was lost in the *Adolfito*, but they say we shall not want any for the rest of our journey, our Indians will hunt on the way. Our launch *Sernamby* from Orton will arrive at the Manú River in two weeks so we shall have only a short canoe journey of 14 days. We can only take very small canoes, the river being so low, so we shall have to repack our big trunks into small ones and only take luggage and provisions, no cargo.

What a time we are having, who would have thought we were going through all this, but still we are seeing something of the world. It is 8 months since we left London and I suppose the first year will have passed before we are settled in Orton. Never mind, we are saving money.

I wish you could see our room, you would pity us, and our small camp beds, with no sheets only a rug. But we are quite used to everything now and think nothing of such things. Our days are always the same. I do a little fancy work [needlework] which I am thankful I brought with me. We read books for the sixth or seventh time. *John Halifax* and the *Golden Butterfly* I think I know by heart.

There are no mosquitos here, but during the day there are thousands of little flies called 'piwns' which bite fearfully and leave tiny black spots, but when it is dark they do not come thank goodness. This is rather a complaining sort of letter, but I am so sick of travelling. Fancy how small a fortnight at the seaside will be after this. I have any amount of dog friends here, I have sometimes 8 or 9 in my room large and small. Then there are some mules which come for a banana every day, and a few ducks and chickens come to pick up bits, so I am not quite deserted.

The children are not very nice, they are so old in their ways, even the baby. There are no children in this country, though people have babies as fast as they can.

Give my love to everybody please and I hope you are all well. I should be rather disappointed if we had to come back now, as much as I long to be with you all, but this is the country to make money and to save it, because there is nothing you can spend it on. Now, goodbye. If Fred has time he is going to make a copy of the map of our journey and send it to Dad.

With best love from us both to you all
Your loving daughter
Lizzie
Love to all. Would Bert still care to come? Fred.

Mishagua, Peru
Monday, 27 September 1897

My dear Dad and Mama,

I am sorry to say we are still here in Mishagua. Fred has done his utmost to get off, but they will give us neither canoes nor men, so here we have to stop until the other partner of this house arrives from Iquitos.

Yesterday we had news from Indians that two launches were coming up, one with the partner and also another gentleman who is interested in our Company and who comes from London. They may arrive here 3 weeks from now, so that is good news for us.

Our people have had to exist on rice and sardines once a day for the last month. We have had just a little better fare being at the house, but not much. They will not sell us anything for love or money. We are all well thank heaven. Fred has had a swollen foot from a bite we think, but it is better now. We have been treated very badly here and we shall make complaints; we think that the lady thinks we are in a way responsible for the death of her husband and she is having a little revenge. Never mind, we shall be all right when the launch arrives.

The Indians are going down river and will take this letter. I hope that the next one will date from Orton. What an expedition this has been, trouble from beginning to end. I only hope that it will finish successfully and the business continue. We know nothing of what is going on, all news having been sent to Orton, the people thinking we have arrived there surely by this time. Our last letters from you were dated February and we received them in Iquitos. I have had the blues dreadfully, there seemed no chance of getting away from here for months, but now we have all cheered up again.

Some of the Indians who have been away rubber cutting arrived here yesterday saying they had been attacked in the forest by the savages. They brought two wounded back with them, one woman shot with an arrow through the two breasts and a man shot in the leg. They managed to kill two of the savages.

Five canoes of them were up here for provisions last week. They were going up one of the rivers to attack smaller tribes, then they capture all the children and sell them as slaves. Three of the slaves of this house, two girls and a boy, ran away a few weeks ago, but they hunted them down and brought them back. They were then chained up that night and the next day beaten until they were so exhausted they did not cry any more, Mrs Fitzcarrald looking on the whole time. She is a brute, I was so sick I had to get away from the house. She now chains them every night to her bed.

She beats all her servants about once a week herself.

The weather is very hot again and we do not go out much except into the forest where it is cool, to catch butterflies. Fred has 200 lovely specimens. In some places in the forest it is very difficult to pass, once we had to walk for half an hour almost always on the top of fallen trees. I shall be able to go in for tight rope walking if this business fails. The forest is beautiful, you would enjoy it, not a sound except the birds and insects and the palms and ferns are grand.

If I could have you all out here I think I should like to stay here always. It is such an easy sort of life, nothing to worry about, dress as you like and do what you like.

But I am longing now for news of you all, fancy being six months without a letter. Orton after this place will be paradise, with the letters coming and going every month, a home of our own, and where we can eat and drink as much as we like.

I must now finish as the Indians must be off. Tell everybody our news and give them all our love. I still keep my diary [now lost] so you can read the history of this eventful year when I return.

I hope you are all as well as we are. With best love from Fred and myself.

Your loving daughter
Lizzie

October is a good month in Mishagua. The river is beginning to rise and a mini-rainy season in the foothills brings a taste of the southern spring.

> Mishagua, Peru
> Monday, 11 October [1897]

My dear Dad and Mama,

At last I can write you the welcome news that on Wednesday we shall start on the last stage of our journey to Orton, where we hope to be at the end of November. Yesterday arrived the partner and his family and since they have been here we have been treated quite differently. He has put himself at our disposal and we can start whenever we like and have everything we want, canoes, Indians, food etc. Also arrived here some soldiers to protect us from the Indians, and a gentleman from the Peruvian Government also came to get all particulars of our expedition and to help

Fred to open up this new road to Bolivia. The government is taking a great interest in us and Fred's name is well known all over these parts. Several accounts have been published in different papers of our sad adventures, etc., but being stuck here we could not get any of them.

When news of Fitzcarrald's death reached Lima it sparked a short-lived interest in the new route, but Peru's capital and Amazon affairs were far apart and the only lasting effect was the name. The route became fixed on the maps as the Isthmus of Fitzcarrald and can be found even in modest atlases – not that anything more than the river exists there now.

Lizzie finished her last letter from Mishagua:

We have had good news of the business and now our future looks much brighter, but the final arrangements we shall hear in Orton.

In Iquitos in the Catholic Church a ceremony was given to rest the souls of our drowned people, a photograph of the decorations was sent us, also memorial cards. We are now working very hard to get off as quickly as possible. We are well, thank heaven, and hope all of you are the same. You will soon hear now of our safe arrival in Orton. I often think how you must worry yourselves and I can hear Dad saying, 'Where is Liz now, and what has she got for dinner.' With best love to all of you from your loving daughter,

Lizzie

Fred sends his love to you all, he is awfully busy now.

If you have any spare patterns of loose blouses, tea gowns, or dressing jackets, should be pleased with them, also a nice turned down collar.

Enclosed feathers from a toucan the Indians shot and we had for dinner.

They left Fitzcarrald's house at the mouth of the Mishagua on 14 October, and the canoes headed upriver for two days. The Mishagua is narrower than the Urubamba, not more than 150 yards wide, and holds much less water. High, forested bluffs stand on each side where mounds of pale earth and rock have been cast down from the Andes. Tiny *quebradas* or gullies open to empty more water from the mountains; some flood only after rain, and the few with permanent water offer un-inviting tunnels into the insect-infested wilderness. Three days up the Mishagua Lizzie and Fred entered a small river coming from the right: the Serjali, not even a hairline on most maps. For hour after hour the river follows an oppressive forest darkened by branches heavy with mosses and ferns. Trees arch the stream and the place seems utterly devoid of human presence. Yet Indians untouched by civilisation, a thought which Lizzie dwelt on briefly in her next letter, are hiding there to this day. It is a lonely, impressive land.

Baradiro, Cwejab River, Peru

Sunday, 31 October [1897]

My dear Dad, Mama and everybody,

We left Mishagua in 5 canoes, 12 Indians and 12 people we were, we have a nice large canoe arranged with a palm leaf *tolda* [a thatched roof awning] to keep the sun off. We were only sorry to leave our poor old dog friends, one of them jumped into the water and tried to swim after us, they will miss us very much; they gave me a little puppy, 4 weeks old, he is blue and very nice, but such a rascal, he bites everything and everybody. He is very particular and when he wanted to go anywhere he insisted on us stopping the canoe, much to the amusement of the Indians.

Well, we had a very rough journey, the water was very low and the weather bad, it rained every night and sometimes we got wet through, beds, rugs, everything. The Indians always made us a tent, but our cover is thin after such rough weather and the rain comes in; very often we had 2 or 3 Indians sleeping under our tent to get out of the rain. The first day we started we found one of our canoes cracked, so we had to unpack it and send down for another. That delayed us 4 hours. There was much dissatisfaction amongst our people the first few days, everybody got so fearfully hungry and we have very few provisions. We could only get a few sardines and some salmon, but we have plenty of rice. We hope to be able to buy something when we get to the Mansi River, but there are no houses the way we have come.

The scenery was grand, the finest we have seen so far. The river is narrow and the trees meet overhead, the sides are high and rocky with plenty of waterfalls and small affluents. The river is very rocky too, and sometimes the Indians had to move the rocks before we could pass. They also had to cut away trees which had fallen across the river and once even had to hew away the rock. We crossed over so many waterfalls. I always stayed in the canoe, but the others had to get out and walk along the shore, sometimes the Indians had to get right under the canoe in the water and lift it bodily. It was fearfully hard work, twice we had to unload them, then they carried luggage and canoes across, reloaded and we went on again. Three days from here we had to change our big canoe for two smaller ones, it could not pass any more. We did a lot of hunting, once we disturbed a herd of 50 wild pigs; they shot two, which we ate. They are very nice. All sorts of lovely birds the Indians shot but we ate them all. Once one shot a monkey and when he picked it up he found a tiny baby one on its back. He gave it to me, but it was too young to feed itself and it died. It is fine to see the Indians catch fish. Sometimes they dive under the water and stay there a long time catching them with a harpoon, or else they shoot them with a bow and arrow. We had plenty of fresh fish. The Indians are very clever and practical people, it seems a shame to interfere and try to civilise them, they are very happy as they are. One of them whilst swimming was attacked by a water pig and had a nasty wound on the head. Fred has taken several photographs with a Kodak which belonged to Dr Vaca Diez, but he is not sure if it takes all right as something snapped inside. We shall be sorry if they are failures. He took me in the canoe passing up a waterfall, also camping out.

We used to bathe in the river at half past five in the morning, have tea and biscuits, start at half past six, travel until ten, have breakfast and dry all our clothes, rugs etc., then travel again until half past five, when we stopped for the night, had dinner, put up beds, tents, etc. It is not bad when the weather is fine, but in wet weather it is very rough travelling; everyone gets cross and tired, and putting up beds and cooking in the rain is not pleasant. We both stand it very well, however, and are in good health. We are enjoying the rest before we go on again. One of our people shot at a large coral snake, 12 feet long, which was hanging over the water. He shot it twice, then it fell into the water. They are very poisonous.

This warm region of the Andean foothills, the so-called *montaña*, supports a rich and varied reptile population comprising many Amazon species together with some from the Andes. A coral snake of the length Lizzie describes is unknown – possibly it was a boa constrictor, or she may simply have exaggerated its size. Dangerous snakes, though, are common, and would have been a serious threat to the expedition as they had to camp each night in freshly cleared forest. Possibly the most fearsome is the *shushupe* or bushmaster, a pit viper up to 11 feet long. Pit vipers have sensitive pits, set just below their eyes, which enable them to sense the presence of prey by detecting its body warmth. Another deadly snake found in these parts, the *fer de lance*, is one of the most feared in the Amazon. Add to these a number of smaller poisonous

75

snakes known by a variety of Indian names, and Fitzcarrald's pass could not have better security.

Again Lizzie mentioned the Mansi River, though the possibility of buying anything there seems most unlikely. The pictures taken on Vaca Diez' Kodak were lost, or more probably never came out. In the heat and humidity both camera and film would have suffered almost instant fungal attack – as Lizzie said, 'a leather toilet bag goes green with mould overnight'.

I shall write a line at every opportunity, but I really think this will be the last before we reach Orton. It really looks as if we are going to get there now, although we have a good 4 weeks journey before us, but we can look back on the worst side now. We shall have been a year travelling, isn't it dreadful? I do wonder what you all think about it; we have got quite used to it now. The only thing that we really long for are nice things to eat sometimes. Fancy living on rice and tinned meat for 6 months. If we do shoot anything it does not go far, we are such a large party, though I, of course, am always served first and best. I am longing to settle down again, anywhere. I don't care where, as long as we can get letters and keep clean again. You have no idea how dirty one gets, the bottom of my dresses and petticoats get fearful from the damp sand and the damp canoe. Going up the falls we always ship water and then it is lovely in the canoe.

Give my love to everybody and tell all who are interested our news, I only write to you at present. I hope Dad got his map all right, he will know where we are now. Fred sends his love to you all, he is very worried, it is no light work to try and make everyone satisfied in the expedition. One wants this and one wants that and they are all so jealous. If Fred talks to one and not the other, they are like a pack of children to manage. I would like to know how my Polly [Lizzie's parrot in England] is, when I get to Orton I will write to Mrs Straker, it is so nice to think that she has a good home. The Indians are waiting to go so I must finish.

Best love to all of you. Think of me when you have your nice Sunday dinners. Dad need not wonder what Liz has got for dinner, because it is either rice and sardines or monkey or parrot.

Lizzie

It took almost three weeks to reach the Isthmus, and when they arrived they camped under a thatched roof, probably a simple shelter made by porters who used the route. Lizzie called the spot the Baradiro. The river here is narrow, no more than 20 feet wide, and jungle pushes in on every side giving an oppressive sense of isolation; the air is filled with the incessant buzz, clatter and scrambling of insects and birds. When Lizzie arrived mules were waiting – they had been taken up by canoe ahead of their party, and were to be kept there for the anticipated cargo boom.

Carefully measured, the distance from one river to the other is less than five and a half miles, a mere nothing in Amazon terms. Without cargo, and allowing for some waist-deep wading, the overland crossing could be shortened to a few yards; but Fitzcarrald had had to choose a route over which boats and supplies could be portaged. Both sides of the Baradiro are roughly 1000 feet above sea level, climbing another 440 feet to the central ridge, with several sharp descents and gullies on the way. With hardly a consideration for the adventure she was having, Lizzie wrote again, this time from the other side.

Baradiro, Caspajali River, Peru
8 November 1897

My dear Dad and Mama,

We have arrived not in Orton but at the other side of the Baradiro. It took us 5 hours to cross over and such a road you cannot imagine, all hills and such steep ones and mud, thick clay, which made it fearfully slippery. The road, as they call it, is simply a narrow path where the trees have been cut down and a good many of them left across the path. Five times we had to cross the river which winds around. I walked for about 1½ hours and then the rest of the journey I rode gentleman fashion on a mule. It was beautiful and I was quite sorry when we came to the end of the journey. He was such a funny old thing he would not keep with the other mules, so we were quite alone. He took not the slightest notice of me, he knew exactly where he had to go and I suppose thought I was a piece of luggage. He stopped to eat when he felt like it and when we came to a very muddy piece of road which he didn't like, he took me into the forest. The consequence was I nearly lost my hat in the trees and the stirrups caught, but I had to pull them out as we went along; he didn't care and wouldn't stop for me. When we came to the river, and he thought the bridge was not strong enough, he climbed down the bank and through the water and up again. At first I was a bit nervous, but I soon found out the way to stick on and he was so surefooted, over trees he went without touching them. If you could only have seen me coming down the steep hills on his back, you would not have slept for a week, and going along narrow paths with steep banks each side; but he did not stumble once, he went along always at the same pace that sometimes I almost forgot I was riding. I had my little dog in front of me too, I had to hold him with one hand.

Mules are wonderful animals and splendid for this country, they can carry heavy cargo too. They had to make 4 journeys to get all our luggage over. At present there are no canoes here, but we have news that in about a week 6 canoes will arrive with rubber and very likely we can use them. It is very unfortunate too that there are no provisions to be had here with the exception of maize, which we have boiled and is very nice; so we have to be careful with the little we have. We have one sack of rice, some salt, a few tins of condensed milk and 1 lb of tea. Meat we have none and have to depend on the hunting. Yesterday they shot a deer, so we have a lovely dinner, the meat is beautiful. I also have in a little private box of my own three good bottles of wine and a bottle of good brandy, a few biscuits and two tins of butter, which we are saving for a rainy day. This is a very poor place, the house is only an open ranch with a good thatched roof in which we have a corner to sleep. Our people have another ranch a little way off, but we are of course received in the house. At meals we have a plate or a spoon, no knives or forks, and one cup for the lot of us. We have to use our own food.

There are any amount of snakes here and yesterday I was sitting in the forest and one came from under my dress. I jumped up quickly and Fred killed it with a stick. We skinned it. There was also one that came after the chickens the other evening. It had two heads, that is instead of a tail it had a head, so if you caught its one head it could attack with the other.

The two-headed snake has appeared in many Amazon adventure stories and comes from the observations of Henry Walter Bates, FRS, whose popular book *The Naturalist on the River Amazons* first appeared in January 1863. Bates travelled for eleven years in the Amazon Basin, much of the time with Alfred Russel Wallace. The two men contributed substantially to the theory of evolution for which Darwin was eventually credited. Some of Lizzie's natural history seems to have been drawn straight from Bates, whose description of an amphisbaena or worm lizard said, 'Their habit of wriggling backwards as well as forwards has given rise to the fable that they have two heads, one at each extremity.' Amphisbaenas are not snakes, as Bates suggested, but more correctly burrowing legless lizards.

The Isthmus was at last behind them, but Lizzie often had no idea of what was to come next. In March she had written saying, 'It will probably be in June before we are in Orton,' and then it was November on the Isthmus. Her clothes must have been thick and fetid with mildew and perspiration. She was certainly fit – though she never mentioned the sores from insect bites that she must have had, or the trombiculid mites that must have left weals up to the waistband of her skirt. These tiny mites, also known as chigger mites, cause intense itching, sometimes accompanied by a fever and more often by sores from scratching to relieve the irritation. The tiny larvae occur in vast numbers in places where the forest has been cleared and then become overgrown. They crawl up travellers' legs until stopped by an obstruction, attaching themselves to the skin and feeding for several days.

The toucan feathers Lizzie sent home were treasured in England by Nell until she died, and when she received them she could never have imagined, in spite of Lizzie's letters, quite what an inhospitable if beautiful region they came from. Lizzie finished her letter:

By the time we reach the Manú River, we hope to meet either a launch or canoes from Orton. I don't know whether I wrote to you that Fred had sent a gentleman a month ago to Orton to fetch a launch and provisions to meet us.

The weather is fearfully hot and flies worry dreadfully, there are no mosquitos, but the small flies which are almost as bad, except that they go away at night. If I can manage it I shall write to Rose, but if I cannot she is sure to read the letters when she comes to see you, as I used to do. I only wish I could come and take tea with you this afternoon, not for the sake of the tea but to see you all again. Never mind, the time will come round soon, we are sure to have a holiday in two years from now and that is not so very long to look forward to. We are very curious to know how things will go when we get to Orton.

Now goodbye, with best love from Fred and myself to all of you.
Your loving daughter,
Lizzie

Chapter Six

'The life in London seems so small after all this'

Bella Vista, meaning Beautiful View, was a *barraca* of Suárez and Fitzcarrald's on the Manú River. There are many Bella Vistas in the Amazon, and most are seen through a haze of midges and other biting insects. In this particular area of jungle it is the *manta blanca*, as the locals say, which falls like a hair shirt over the river. Every square inch of exposed skin gets bitten; there is no escape, and Lizzie could only hope that it would be better in Orton. 'We left the Baradiro a fortnight ago and came *down* the Caspajali river, one day's canoe trip to this place . . .' Lizzie underlined 'down' to emphasise the change of direction: they were now flowing with the river, and making good speed. 'We have a faint ray of hope of getting to Orton by Xmas,' she wrote on 8 December.

They sat looking out at the forest. Mist filled the trees, then sunlight and, by the afternoon, rain. For the first time the full implications of the loss of the *Adolfito* and the death of Vaca Diez hit Lizzie, and her thoughts became anxious. Would they have to make their way back over the Isthmus and down the Urubamba rapids? Who in London would take over the reins of the company now that Francisco Suárez was dead? It would soon be a year since his death and they had not heard anything. 'For a whole week I had the blues dreadfully,' Lizzie said. 'We did not know what was going to become of us and you were all getting ready for Xmas.' The days passed slowly at Bella Vista until a canoe arrived.

> Yesterday a special messenger arrived in a canoe with a telegram for Fred, to say that he was to carry out his business just the same, the death of Vaca Diez making no difference to the Company, so we think that our future will be safe now.

The telegram reached Pará on the cable of the Eastern Telegraph Co., then went by steamer to Iquitos – the Pará to Manaus link was temporarily broken. Lizzie takes up the story again:

> They had chartered a special steamer to bring the telegram to Mishagua and from there a special messenger in a canoe. We were all in high spirits at the news and finished the day in a very jolly manner. We had all had the blues most fearfully, thinking the

Company had smashed and we were deserted in this savage part, but now we have all cheered up and are going to try and have a good day of it.

Bella Vista is near the head of the Manú River, now one of the few remaining places in the Amazon where wildlife is abundant. In the 1890s, though, the Manú was frontier country in the commercial battle for rubber supremacy. *Seringueiros* had settled along the river, Indians were hunted for labour, and *bolachas* of rubber were piled high on the banks. Writing from Bella Vista, Lizzie said:

Well, we then came here in some canoes which had brought rubber up; that was a quiet trip, we started at 11 o'clock and got here at 6 in the evening. We saw plenty of snakes in the water, so it is not safe to bathe any more. Fred had a letter of introduction to the gentleman here, so we were received nicely. It is a large house or ranch, built above the ground. We share a room with 2 gents belonging to the house and eat with them too; they only have rice and bananas, but always send an Indian out hunting, so three times a week we have either fish, monkey or birds; there is not a scrap of sugar to be had. I have a little box full which I keep on the quiet, but the others have to drink their tea and coffee without; we still have a little tea and coffee left. We have been here 3 weeks waiting for canoes, they were all away collecting rubber; yesterday a gent arrived with 3 which he has put at our disposal, also with the news that our launch must be at the mouth of the Madre de Dios by this time. So we leave here on Tuesday and go down the Manú River for 4 days to Panagua where we hope to meet our launch. If not we must wait until it does come, or news from Orton, as the Indians do not like to go into the Madre de Dios on account of the savages.

Everyone respected the Madre de Dios River. Starting as a web of small streams only 100 miles from the Inca city of Cuzco, it has grown into a 200-yard-wide monster by the time the Manú appears. Faustino Maldonado, a Peruvian explorer, followed its length in 1861 and reached the Madeira Falls, where he drowned. Another early expedition never even got that far, being slaughtered by Indians on the banks.

Lizzie and Fred had to travel down much of its formidable course to reach the Beni, and they could have expected an attack at any time because they were travelling close to the shore. So as they waited in the Manú they would have been justifiably apprehensive: with range upon range of the Andes on one side, and the rapids of the Madeira on the other, they were well beyond the reach of law and order. From Bella Vista Lizzie wrote:

> There is a large slave trade carried on in these parts, a strong healthy girl costs £50. All your servants you have to buy, they are all kidnapped children, people bring them up and when they are about 14 years, sell them for enormous prices. When you buy them they are your own property and have to work as hard as you like to make them, and if they don't work well, they are beaten dreadfully. Even the men have 50 or 100 strokes sometimes, with a stick which cuts like a knife and very often are half dead afterwards. If they try to run away they are punished more for that than anything else.

Somewhere along the way the English doctor stayed behind.

> When we have finished with this country I don't think I shall ever want to travel any more, I had more than I bargained for this time. I feel the want of a companion very much sometimes, and wish there were a few English people with us. There is only an engineer and he is such a fearful Cockney. I mustn't talk to him much or else the others are jealous. They are like a pack of children. Fred and I have to be so careful to smile at them all. We wish we had Nell with us to play 'Muggem' and Ludo or 'things in the room' or something or other. Fancy, a whole year with nothing to do. Well, it is nearly over now and I hope we shall find some papers and books in Orton, if they haven't been stolen; this is a fearful country for stealing, old and young, masters and men take everything they can get hold of. We have quite made up our minds that if everything goes on alright here, we shall come home the Spring after next for a holiday and then come out again for another 3 years and then home for good.
>
> Now goodbye, send me all spare papers and books and write to me as often as you can. With love to all of you from Fred and myself.
>
> Your loving daughter Lizzie

By the time she wrote again it was Christmas Day. They celebrated at Colón, a *barraca* on the right bank of the Manú River. Parties in out-of-the-way reaches of the Amazon have a style of their own, demanding a strong stomach and even stronger legs. The idea seems to be to throw down as much *aguardiente* as the central nervous system will stand. The primitive rites of an Amazon drinking competition begin with the command '*Al seco*' – 'To the last drop' – usually shouted by anyone who is actually sober at the start. Small glasses – roughly a good double measure by most conventions – are downed in one gulp. Then the cry 'Al seco' goes up again, and so on. Ladies generally retire early, and sleep fitfully as the Al secos echo through the forest. Stumbling in the dark and swearing fearfully, the revellers fall into hammocks or the river. Although she gives no details, Fred and Lizzie's Christmas sounds as though it followed this tradition.

Colón, Manú River, Peru
Christmas Day [1897]

My dear Dad, Mama and everyone,

How I wish I was with you today! You will think of us I am sure and wonder where we are.

We have been here 2 weeks today, at a ranch belonging to an awfully nice Peruvian rubber man and on the whole we are not badly off and have actually managed an Xmas dinner. We bought a fowl and some eggs and to drink we have the rum made from sugarcane which is awfully strong. We started last night already, had speeches, fired shots off and were really jolly. The consequence is the gents are in bed this morning to get fresh again for this evening.

Without help, Amazon travel becomes tedious and difficult. Hospitality is customary and, then as now, Lizzie found people generous most of the time.

Mostly they bring back monkeys, but a few days ago they brought a wild pig. We tried hard to buy a turkey, which belongs to a man in one of the other ranches, but he would not sell it. We even stole it but he managed to get it back again, so we have to be content with our fowl and monkeys.

It seems out of character for Lizzie to resort to stealing, but homesickness for her family and for a traditional Christmas may have distorted her natural sense of right or wrong. However, that sort of problem was the exception and, as she said,

They always gave me something, eggs, beans or onions; we did not live so badly on this voyage. The Indians caught plenty of fish.

In the Manú, as in other Amazon rivers, fish are plentiful, and the local Indians know many ways to catch them. A bow and arrow is used for fish in shallow water or just under the surface. Arrows for fishing have specially light shafts so that they float in the event of a miss. Alternatively the Indians of the Manú, like many of the local tribes, use a poison produced by mashing a certain forest vine. Thrown into slow-flowing or calm water, the poison paralyses the fish and they float to the surface. Lizzie would have seen many curious fish taken from the

Manú, including voracious pirañas with their razor-sharp teeth, and armoured catfish, their heads covered by tough plates and their mouths surrounded by long, whisker-like barbels.

None of the letters described fish and Lizzie hardly ever mentioned the river dangers, not even in comments about bathing. Everyone takes care to avoid shallows unless the water has been disturbed, as one particular ray found in these places causes more injuries than most other Amazon denizens combined. Lizzie's almost casual approach is surprising, and though she may not have been concerned she would have been told to take care. Even in those days the rubber men would have joked about the tiny, almost transparent *candirú* catfish which homes in on a stream of urine and heads straight into the most delicate of burrows. Once inside, the *candirú* is stuck because of the backward-facing spines around its head.

> There are about 100 rubber gatherers scattered about this part, so it is a little bit lively. They are all nice, kind people, but of course a little bit rough . . . they make very nice honey from the sugar cane and which we put in our tea or coffee, instead of sugar (of which we have none). I like to eat it with the bananas too.

As Lizzie discovered, sugar, even the coarse brown variety, is not a local product. Upriver, the juice from sugar cane is reduced by boiling, then left to cool when it becomes a hard brown block.

Surprising, too, is the way in which bananas can take the place of staples such as potatoes and rice. When toasted, one of the semi-sweet varieties makes delicious breadcrumbs, which are used to coat meat before frying. As a truly exotic dish, nothing can beat a slice of paca, a large jungle rodent, rolled in these breadcrumbs and gently fried in peccary lard. Travellers' praises in the Amazon never change, and Lizzie's delight was typical.

> There are large banana plantations here, with 4 kinds of banana. There are bread bananas, which they roast in the ashes and is very dry and we eat with our coffee in the morning; then there is a large sweet banana which also has to be cooked and is eaten with meat; then there is the apple banana which is eaten raw and tastes like apples; and the small sweet banana like you get in Europe. Then they have haricot beans which grow here and *yuca* plant, the root of which is eaten and is something like potatoes; we are better off here than we have been for sometime.

Even in the distant Manú life was looking up, and though they had to wait before continuing downstream to Panagua Lizzie was brighter. Being a lady and the wife of a *patrón*, she commanded respect and was helped; that she explains on several occasions. But in no way should her personal stoicism and determination be underestimated. The upper reaches of the Manú and the Isthmus of Fitzcarrald are no place for anyone in their right mind even now. Almost every expedition there in recent times has been attacked; some of the people involved in the filming of the German director Werner Herzog's *Fitzcarraldo* were shot with arrows by a hostile tribe who resented their intrusion. Fred marked the tribes on his map, and on the left bank of the Manú he wrote on 'Amahuacas'; they are there today and have attacked outsiders. On the right bank of the river when Fred and Lizzie were there the tribes may have been Masco or just possibly a few of the Huachipari; both led simple, uncomplicated lives reliant on the forest storehouse. As the *caucheros* moved in, some Indians were forced out and others of different tribes brought in.

. . . after our good news I am all right again and hope to really be in Orton by the end of January, when we can at last settle down and be comfortable and get news from you all. I know you must be anxious when you don't get letters, but you need not worry any more, for our luck has turned and the rest of our journey we make in the launch, so there is no fear of the Indians, because they are afraid of it and run away. I hope you have received all my letters. I have written from every place, but the letters have mostly been entrusted to Indians, so I do not know if they will reach you safely.

What a journey we have made and what we have seen! The life in London seems so small after all this. I am sorry Bert was not with us, he would have enjoyed it, although for me it was a bit too hard. Everyone thinks I have been through it well and bravely, but I did not think about it at all; in fact I rather enjoyed the dangerous parts. I wish you could have seen me riding on the mule, that was the best sight.

If the photos turn out all right they will give you an idea of the journey, but I am afraid the dampness will spoil them. All our books which we brought out are ruined, but our other things are in fairly good condition. My album is quite good. I always keep that handy to have a look at you all now and again. My little dog is growing nicer every day and is a nice amusement for us, he is a favourite everywhere and bosses all other dogs, big and little.

Tell Nell to write to me all about Xmas and her secrets, and everyone else must write sometimes, you don't know how the slightest bit of news from Europe cheers us up. I do hope you are all well at home and everything going on the same way. We keep very well and stand the heat splendidly, we are only lazy through having nothing to do for such a long time.

Now goodbye, with best love to all of you and wishing you all a Happy New Year from both Fred and myself,

Your loving daughter,

Lizzie

Halfway down the Manú the river is between 50 and 100 yards wide. Rich forest with tangles of lianas competing for light crowds the banks. A booming roar of howler monkeys grows as the troop passes, and then dies away until lost among other jungle noise. King vultures flop among the branches above a fetid corpse, while caimans slip from the banks silently if they can, or with a sudden plop if surprised. From the right bank the Panagua River comes in with water drained from the Andean slopes. In late January both rivers are rising quickly to reach their top level, and at that time of year launches often reached Panagua, a small *barraca* where Lizzie and Fred had to wait again.

Panagua, Manú River, Peru

11 January 1898

My dear Dad and Mama,

We are waiting, waiting, waiting, but we are both well and hope you are all well.

We have news of the launch, but if it is true we do not know, such awful reports get about. I should not be a bit surprised if someone told you we had been drowned with the others, the people here are fearful liars. The two Indians who went to Orton with one of our gents to fetch the launch passed by in a canoe during the night, someone met them upriver, otherwise we should have known nothing about it. They say that there are 3 launches coming, which will arrive in 2 or 3 days, but as they were alone in a canoe and brought no letter, it looks very much as if they had turned away, especially as they passed at night, so we do not know whether to believe it or not; we can only hope and wait. These Indians are such funny people, you can get nothing out of them and we know they are afraid of the launches now, their *patrón* having been drowned in one. We hope to reach Orton some day or other. It is about time, don't you think?

Lizzie sat and wrote during the days of rain, insects and thoughts of Indians. She had time to pass on a message for Nell: 'I wish her Many Happy Returns – yesterday.' Nell was then thirteen, and soon Lizzie and Fred would have been married five years.

Tell Bert we are still hoping that we can have him come out, we want one of the family badly – of course he would not come this way and Fred or someone would meet him somewhere or other. We shall have heaps of commissions for him, things which we want badly.

Enforced idleness is never good and the Amazon is a firm master. Without a canoe one's thoughts turn to other ways of escape, but rafts can be wet and go only at the speed of the current – perhaps 3 miles an hour. To reach Orton from Panagua would take weeks. Lizzie simply waited, resigned and with few complaints, and most of all she missed contact with her family.

We have learned to be patient in this country and how to travel. When I think of the fuss we used to make preparing to go to the sea, I have to laugh.

If we were not so anxious we should not be having a bad time of it here, we live fairly well and I always have my afternoon cup of tea. In the evening we play poker. I have not much news this time, the life here is the same day after day, the only excitement is when someone arrives or goes away.

Fred sends his love to all of you, he will be glad to be at work again. How is Polly? I expect she is spoilt by them all. Remember us to the Straker family please, I am so thankful that Polly found such a good home. I am longing to have a menagerie again.

Now, goodbye, with love to all from,

Your loving daughter,

Lizzie

When many would have given up and started to plant the next season's *yuca*, the launch arrived, five weeks after they had crossed the Isthmus. From Panagua Lizzie wrote her longest letter. She had heard from home, including news of her brother Fred who had been working in Mexico. She saw the *Morning Leader* article by 'Marie' for the first time. Also for the first time she met Nicholás Suárez – he brought the launch *Esperanza* from his *barraca*, El Carmen, on the Madre de Dios.

Panagua, Manú River, Peru
Monday, 7 February 1898

My dear People,

Off my head, launch arrived, brought letters, also provisions, also director, there is a place called Orton, we get there in 2 weeks. Now I have let off a little steam I will tell you my news. The fact of the matter is, when we least expected it, bang came a launch steaming round the corner. It was such a surprise, although we have been waiting weeks for it, but we had given up all hope of anything good in this world, especially as we had had a funeral here in the morning. One of the Indians died of dysentry and we consequently had the hump, but I suppose that was the last but one straw, so it did not break the camel's back. Well, I think I told you a few years or weeks or days ago, that Francisco Suárez, one of the Directors, had died in London. Well his brother, who is a big man in these parts, has taken his share and so went to Orton, saw how things were and then came in his launch, the *Esperanza*, to fetch us. So thank heaven we shall leave here in 5 days and have a fairly comfortable journey of only 2 weeks to Orton. He says that the business in Orton is good, but was near failing on account of the heavy expenses of the expedition (about £20,000 loss). They are, however, anxiously waiting for Fred to arrive to finally take over the business. He says the house which we shall have is furnished, and the finest in all these rivers, so we hope to be a bit comfortable.

We shall have no fear of the savages now, as they run away from the launch.

Well I think I also told you a few centuries ago that the two Indians who went to Orton to fetch the launch came back alone in a canoe. They told us that they were attacked by the savages and had lost a large packet of letters, which they were bringing to us from Orton, but it turns out now that they ran away not wanting to come in the launch, so their tale was a fib. We have received several letters from you all up to dates June and July, and we sat up nearly all night reading and studying them, and I was so excited I could not sleep a wink. It is exactly one year since I received news from you, only fancy. I am so thankful that you are all well, that is the first thing to set my mind at rest. Tell Bib to write me plenty of letters after the same style as last, we roared over them. I am not going to answer any of them now, but wait until we get to Orton, as you will very likely receive letters from there before you get this. Have received 3 letters from you, which my dear Mum made me wish I could come home for a week or two. I do long for a sight of you all now and again. Had also letters from Alice and Rosie, there must be plenty more waiting for us in Orton.

Also had a good laugh over the article in the *Morning Leader*. I think I could give her something really interesting to write about now, don't you? We are both very well, although I had an attack of dysentry, but I went to bed and kept warm, which is really the only cure and to starve yourself, which the Indians will not do. Of course, you feel awfully hungry, so they eat and eat and the poor things have to keep running out during the night in the heavy dew, so they have not much chance of getting well. Exposing themselves like that nearly always brings on inflamation and then they die quickly. The only thing is to starve and to keep warm and you are quickly well. It is really the only complaint, except a sort of ague fever which comes on through catching cold and being careless and then is very difficult to get rid of; it lasts for years, coming on regularly at the same hour every third day and lasts for 3 hours. Two of our people have it. We both know perfectly how best to take care of ourselves in this climate, consequently we are both well.

Tell Dad from Orton I am sending him a complete map of our route, marking all the places we have stopped at. I wish he would write me a line now and again on Sundays.

As Lizzie promised, Fred drew a rough sketch map on the back of one of the letters. It marked two routes across the divide from the Urubamba River – Fred called one of them the 'old way', and it used a crossing from another tributary to Camisea. And though John Mathys would not have had any idea of the kind of place it was, he could possibly have guessed that his daughter was indeed among the first across.

I am sure your garden must be nice and allow me to inform you I am going to have a tropical garden in Orton, shall send you a picture of it. The orchids are about in thousands, they grow on old sticks, in fact everywhere, but at present are not in bloom.

We have been eating all sorts of strange animals and been jolly glad to get them, such as wild rats, a splendid meat; monkeys large and small, all kinds and conditions of birds, wild pigs, deer, tortoises, squirrels etc. etc. I have a baby pigeon which my doggie caught in the forest and I have to feed him 3 times a day with soft food on the end of a spoon, he is getting quite tame. The Indians are very fond of taking whole nests full of young birds and bringing them up, they all get so tame and walk about the house and wherever they like, all sorts of birds, large and small. They are very fond of both birds and animals and treat them kindly.

Poor old Fred [Lizzie's brother], came home to see you, wasn't he surprised to hear of another traveller in the family. You must tell him all my news until he is settled for good somewhere, when I shall write to him regularly. Does he speak Spanish? I am getting on nicely, we shall be able to *parlez-vous* when we meet again. My Fred speaks perfectly now, he has been right through the grammar

3 times and reads only Spanish books. I plod along slowly, but I think I shall get there! Tell Bert to study Spanish if he has time. Shall answer all your letters thoroughly from Orton. Tell Bib the director who came to fetch us is a millionaire, but I shall keep my eyes open. She ought to send me a fascinating picture of herself to exhibit through *à la Morning Leader*.

Now goodbye my dear people, think of me, write to me, don't forget me, send books to me, papers to me, dream of me and all the rest of me.

Love to all, with one united call,

Yours affectionately,

Lizzie

Queen of Orton (Bolivia) Rubber Company

Oh, please, my silver you are taking care of, ask one of the girls to clean it about once every three months and charge a commission.

I do not think we shall want it for at least 5 years.

From Panagua to the Boca del Manú, literally the mouth of the River Manú, to the Madre de Dios was one long day's journey. The first night they felt safe to shelter by the entrance of a small *cocha*, part of the old river channel. Then they made full steam ahead for Orton, keeping to the middle of the river whenever possible.

At this point the Madre de Dios is still moving fast, almost visibly downhill at times. It is up to 300 yards wide in some places, with broad, shallow, curving bends and trees on every horizon. The Madre de Dios is the most impressive river in that part of Peru; occasionally the bank is high – perhaps 150 feet of orange earth as a reminder that the mountains are not far away, though it is not long before the river settles into an easy flow broken only by forested islands and narrow channels. Most wildlife keeps to the forest, as did the Indians in Lizzie's day. Caimans, some ten feet long or more, were common on the Madre de Dios even in the mid-1960s, but then the skin traders moved in. At the turn of the century the trade goods were different too, as Lizzie's record confirms.

I am sure Dad is waiting for news of the savages; well the second day in the Madre de Dios we saw 3 men, but they only came out of the forest after we had passed. We suppose they came to look at the launch. But we have several little savage boys on the launch which had only been captured a few days, we were taking them for sale to another village.

In the Madre de Dios at that time the Indians were mostly Tacanans, all related by language though split into many small tribal groups. They lived together, two to eight families in one hut with a communal chief.

They used powerful six-foot palmwood bows and fired arrows tipped with the iron-like *chonta*. Each arrow, made of cane, had a flight of two twisted half-feathers set spirally against the shaft and fixed by a binding of native cotton thread – simple technology, but deadly. One of these arrows could penetrate an inch-thick plank at 30 yards; and there are some good stories, which may or may not be true, of arrows piercing the metal sides of launches. Lizzie and Fred were lucky. No showers of arrows thudded into the boat and, as Lizzie said, the Indians kept away – they were curious but afraid, in much the same way as the last of the Amazon's uncontacted tribes watch modern light aircraft.

In the capable hands of Suárez the very last lap of the journey to Orton turned out to be uneventful. He knew how to handle most problems, and it was in many ways his river: in the negotiations with Fitzcarrald Suárez had offered to keep out of the Manú if Fitzcarrald left him the Madre de Dios. When first explored, it had been described as one of the richest regions in the world for coffee, cocoa, quinine, gold and rubber. With such temptations not even hostile Indians could keep the pioneers out for long. Suárez and Fitzcarrald were not alone – French, Germans and Peruvians went to the Madre de Dios, though they presented no competition to Suárez.

The *Esperanza* crossed the current and headed towards the right bank of the Beni and the tiny settlement. A few houses set on a 30-foot-high bank had been there since 1884, when it was a *barraca* called La Cruz, or Ribera Alta, the high bank. When Lizzie arrived, the town of Riberalta, with a population of 252, had been officially established for only three years. They were guests of the French house of Braillard, another trade pioneer, and, as Lizzie said, 'We slept 2 nights and had a gay time . . . the consequence was we did not get up in time to catch the launch and she arrived in Orton without us.' They were later told how they had missed a splendid reception given in their honour as survivors of the Urubamba disaster. There were flags on the buildings and lights in the trees, everybody wore their best clothes and the Orton workforce had been given the day off. Everyone who owned a gun had turned out to fire the welcoming salute. And Lizzie and Fred had been left behind in Riberalta!

Lizzie, again unconcerned, said that Orton was just two hours away downriver, so they found a boat and set off in the late afternoon, fully experienced after all their adventures. 'We arrived in a small boat late at night, in a bad thunderstorm, nobody expecting us – Mathys luck,' Lizzie wrote. This must have been an unnerving experience. Storms on jungle rivers are never to be taken lightly as the sudden wind whips up huge waves. The storm occurred during the end of the first week of March 1898. They had been travelling for almost thirteen months and had survived one of the longest river journeys ever made, some 4000 miles.

Chapter Seven

'Queen of Orton'

Orton
11 March 1898

My dear People,

I think when I wrote my last letter, I was off my head. Well, I have now recovered and we are actually in Orton . . .

Orton was the finest *barraca* in the Beni, and so unique that it appears on only a handful of maps. Vaca Diez began to build it in the early 1880s, and by the time Lizzie and Fred arrived it was a thriving concern. The site chosen by Edwin Heath was perfect: a 30-foot-high bluff on the Beni, close to the mouth of the Orton River, with excellent rubber forest on the doorstep and good access to two rivers. On one side flowed the Beni, almost 400 yards wide, sluggish and gentle, while the much narrower Orton meandered at the back door. Having claimed the spot, Vaca Diez built well, and Orton became a legend along the river. Ten years before Lizzie arrived the place was visited by a Brazilian, Coronel Antonio Labre, who said, 'We were received by Dr Antonio Vaca Diez, a Bolivian senator who has a large settlement there and employs 300 workmen.' At about the same time an American pharmacist, a Mr H. Rusby, travelling for Parke, Davis & Co. of Detroit to collect forest plants, called at Orton; Rusby later recollected how Vaca Diez was known as the King of the Beni.

When Vaca Diez drowned in the Urubamba Señora Lastenia, his wife, was living in Hampstead with her children, so it was Lizzie who assumed the vacant 'throne'.

> . . . after all the tumbledown places we have lived in, we expected a respectable-looking hut, but nothing of the kind, there is a most beautiful house of 2 storeys, with a wide balcony all round the house, about six rooms upstairs, but tremendous. We have two of them, the others are kept for visitors, of which there are many passing through and stopping perhaps for a couple of days. Down below are the offices, one for the clerks and one for Fred (where I am writing my letter), also there are the shops and warehouses, everything beautifully arranged; the corridors downstairs are inlaid with tiles and there is everything we can possibly want

except a dub [lavatory] in the house; there is one, the first we have met for some months, but it is some distance from the house.

Mr Arnold, the managing clerk, here with his wife (a Bolivian) have another house not anything like ours but very nice too. We dine with them and the clerks also dine there in another room. I have nothing at all to do with the meals.

There are also several other small houses for clerks and the work people of the estate. So far we have had plenty of fresh meat and milk. Every morning at 7 o'clock they send to our rooms, chocolate, milk, bread and biscuits. We then take our baths in our bedroom. Fred goes down to his office. I potter about my rooms with my swell tea gown on, at 12 o'clock we go to the other house for lunch and a fine meal too. In the afternoon I sit with Mrs Arnold for a couple of hours trying to speak Spanish. At 6 we take our dinner, then promenade or talk. Once we danced with a concertina for the band; there is no piano at present.

Such was the drive of pioneering in the Amazon that even pianos were shipped from Europe to some of the most out-of-the-way places. One traveller, F. Keller, who was on the route before the rubber boom, said: 'Packages of from 500–600 lbs are sometimes transported to Bolivia in the same covers in which they came from Pará; and I was told that even pianos have been thus conveyed, and wonderful to relate – have arrived entire at Santa Cruz de la Sierra.' Santa Cruz is over 500 miles beyond Orton, on one of the headwaters of the River Mamoré.

I have a manservant, he has his hammock up on the balcony and is at my disposal the whole of the day. He cleans my rooms, arranges my bath, etc. etc. We are great swells; the people treat us most respectfully. I think we shall have a very pleasant life here and I do not think we shall have to spend much money, as we get everything free, washing included. The only thing is it is a very thirsty country and everything is so terribly dear, for a bottle of beer 10/–, a bottle of brandy 20/– etc. etc. The water is very good though, there is a spring close by.

I have so much to tell you that I do not know what to write first. I must put the things down as they come into my head. We have not very much furniture in our rooms at present, but there is a carpenter's shop with 6 men and they are to make us some; we have a good bed though and a very nice settee and half a dozen chairs and one or two tables. The floor is covered with an ornamental matting, very nice and cool; all the windows have nice white curtains. Mrs Arnold has been to Germany with her husband so she knows how to make things nice. It is so beautiful to settle down again after 15 months travelling. I am so tired I cannot rest enough and, not being used to the good food, the second day I had a grand bilious attack, but on the whole we are both very well. It is a great pity that there is no regular post here. For 3 months they have not received letters, so I did not find many waiting for me here, but I had a few from you dear Mum, and from Bib. I enjoy her letters and read extracts from them to some of the gents. They were greatly amused at her idea of life here, such as wearing trousers, hair cut short, etc. Please Bib cheer me up often, I do feel lonely sometimes with so much Spanish. I also heard from Jack, Rosie and Alice. I only received 4 magazines but expect others when they send for the post. I have given orders for a special post service to be arranged. I would like very much to have some fashion books and patterns as I shall have to make all my clothes myself.

There is another Bolivian lady here, the wife of a Captain. She understands dressmaking a little, but they are anxious for new patterns. All the other women are workpeople. For the meals they are arranging a sort of hotel and the French cook and his wife who came with us are to manage everything, so I shall have nothing to do but arrange my rooms and enjoy myself.

Lizzie soon discovered how business and politics were intermingled in the bustling life of Orton. To further his political intentions Vaca Diez published a newspaper, *La Gaceta del Norte*, the only one in the area. It offered local news in tabloid style, mixed with advertisements and gleanings of overseas affairs taken from letters – some, probably, from the Mathys family.

While the *barraca* itself was a self-contained, well-ordered concern, it was the centre of an empire of which few outsiders had any knowledge, even if they had read Coronel Labre's account. The Orton River was navigable by *lanchas* for 50 miles, and by large canoes for 100 more. Then within the Vaca Diez sphere of influence another river, the Abuna, could be reached by trails cut through the forest; and beyond that lay the prize, the River Acre, with the richest rubber in the Amazon. With ruthless determination Vaca Diez had established many outposts and planned to use his fresh capital to 'consolidate', which among rubber pioneers meant to take over, buy out or force out the small operator by any method. Such tactics did not escape Lizzie.

I must tell you how they do business here. This house and another house wanted to buy a large rubber plantation a few days off. The man was here, the other house took possession of him, made him drunk and locked him up until the papers for the sale were read. Our people captured him, kept him drunk and locked him up here for 2 weeks and he signed papers selling his business to us. In the meantime the other people went off armed and took possession of his estate, so a few days ago a lot of our people with Indians all armed and with the owner of the estate went off to turn them out. They say it will come to fighting; that's the way they manage things here. The estate is a valuable one and the law counts for nothing in these parts, everyone looks after himself.

That deal meant another pin in the company map behind Mr Arnold's desk. Consolidation also meant better rivercraft, trading centres, collecting points and guards. There were Europeans at some of the outposts, and in Orton itself a strong community spirit, which made life more pleasant for the sociable Lizzie. Her only complaint was the postal service; everything came over the Madeira Falls a short way downriver – there were inevitable losses and delays for the 'budgets', once landed in San Antonio. Even so, letters posted from London usually reached her within three months; but it still represented an exasperating wait for Lizzie. Her anxious request that her family check the way they address their letters to her is understandable.

The mail came in but brought no letters from any of you, only two Xmas cards from Mrs Limberger [Fred's aunt] and Melchior [Fred's London tailor]. I cannot understand it, and I received no papers or books, I was dreadfully disappointed. Goodness knows when the next batch of letters will come. Do you address your letters as the following?
Mrs Hessel,
Orton Rubber Co.,
Orton,
Bolivia, S A
Via Pará and S. Antonio
The mail service is simply dreadful. When we do get letters they arrive with all the stamps torn off and part of the envelopes too.

As letters, magazines and newspapers arrived they were devoured page after page – first by Lizzie and her friends, and then by termites and ants. Among the first mail from home Lizzie received news of Queen Victoria's Diamond Jubilee which had been celebrated the previous June, while they were waiting at the Tambo River. The cover of the *Illustrated London News* was suitably royal, with its undisguised promotion for the Empire – it all seemed so remote from Orton.

Above By the time Lizzie reached
the heavily-forested Andean foothills,
she had crossed the continent.
Lizzie found much excitement among
the rapids and waterfalls in this section
of the river

Previous page Well upriver, close to
the Andes, some Amazon tributaries

have narrowed to small streams. 'The
river is very rocky,' wrote Lizzie, 'and
sometimes the Indians had to move the
rocks before we could pass'

Inset In narrow places where the forest
closes in on every side, dead wood and
debris mark the level of the annual flood

Above *The geometric designs of the Shipibo Indians are painted with natural pigments. When Lizzie passed through Shipibo country in 1897, these people had known little contact with outsiders*

Left *The customs of Campa Indians living in remote parts of the upper Amazon in Peru have changed little since Lizzie's time. Maize ground to a pulp is chewed, then spat into a trough; water is added and fermentation to an alcoholic porridge takes about twelve hours*

Right *At Panagua on the River Manú, an early morning mist hangs in the forest until cleared by the sun's warmth. By noon the mood can change again with sudden storms and heavy rain*

Overleaf *Canoes hollowed from a single trunk are the least expensive and most convenient personal boats on the upper Amazon*

Above *Edwin Heath, an American explorer, chose this high bluff for Vaca Diez on 9 October 1880, marking a tree with his name. On the same day he reached the mouth of a tributary and named it the Orton, after an American university teacher and explorer named James Orton. The trees are mangoes, which are thought to have been planted by Vaca Diez as an avenue leading to the Barracon, as the great house is remembered*

Below *The Tahuamanu was new when Lizzie was in Orton, and was mentioned on the last page of the Gaceta on 1 December 1899, just before she died. This lancha formed part of the small fleet which ferried President General Don José Manuel Pando to the Acre in the war of 1903*

[Orton]
15 March 1898

It is 3 days ago since the first page of my letter was written; somehow the time passes so quickly I can do nothing. I am sure the next 4 years will slip by before we know where we are. Well, I must tell you that yesterday we christened one of the new launches. We all went on board and had champagne, etc., and in the evening we had a ball in one of the large rooms of our house; for the orchestra we had an accordian and flute, but sorry to say we were only four ladies (poor ladies). We had to dance each dance with three or four different gents; there were about forty gents. I had to fly to my bedroom to breathe now and again, but on the whole we enjoyed ourselves. Some gents could dance, and some thought they could, whilst others apologised before they started (my poor trilbies [feet]). I do wish I had some of my beautiful sisters here. There is an English gent in the next city, town or village, who gets all sorts of magazines and papers from England, he sent me down a tremendous bundle yesterday, also some fine novels.

There are heaps of people here at present; sometimes I don't know where I am, the only time I get to myself is the morning. I struck for my tea in my rooms, so I can have two or three hours alone. I have got my rooms pretty straight now; I wish you could see them, there is a sort of dresser arrangement in my bedroom which I have converted into a dressing table, it looks A1.

All our sufferings seem to be over now, the people here do everything they can to make us comfortable; neither of us seem to have any bad effects from the journey. I soon get tired, is the only thing, but I am taking a tonic and will soon get fat again. I am truly thankful that you are all well and only wish you could all come and pay me a visit. How Dad would enjoy looking about at the different arrangements, he would not say 'poor Liz' any more. I have given information to all the likely people I meet that I adore animals, so I have various promises of crocodiles, snakes, cockroaches and other sweet creatures for my menagerie. As soon as we have settled down thoroughly we shall see about sending photographs of our house, etc. By the bye I have not received the photographs of Bib and Lou, perhaps it is a good thing as I am not very strong at present and the shock might be too great (dear girls).

Tell Dad when we come home with our fortune???? he shall take the whole lot of his animals to his home, mother, father, uncles, aunts etc. etc. Fred and I always wanted to go badly. I mean to go to Switzerland, of course.

I shall not turn up my nose at your forests and rivers, my dear people. Here they are grand to look at, but you cannot walk in them without getting covered with insects and spiders and awful wood lice, and looking out for snakes, etc. the whole time; and as for sitting down in them, impossible. I have had to go in for corsets again; here we have always to be dressed swell on account of the visitors always coming. I have some awfully pretty dresses, sea green, cream, pink, blue, etc. all pretty but £11 washing stuffs. I wish I had brought some lace collars, I have two and they are so convenient to wear with the different dresses. If anyone comes out they will have heaps of shopping to do for us.

I have all the jubilee papers, but have not had time to look at them; it must have been a grand affair though. Fred has not sent his report off yet, but we think it will be favourable; he has to see the other estates yet. It is almost sure that we shall stay here for another 4 years, but if we can manage a holiday before, we shall do so. It is very difficult to leave a business like this as the people do not work unless you look after them. I have the same thing with my man 'Daniel'! I have to show him where the dusty corners are, etc. Every morning I have to tell him what to do, the people here cannot think for themselves. I do not know if I have told you enough of our life here, if there is anything special you want to know, you must ask me. I am drinking lemon water whilst I am writing, there are heaps of lemons for a poor bilious subject. Please tell me everything that goes on, I long to hear of you all. Nell has not written to me yet. Tell her to learn as much as she can at school and when I come home for a holiday, if she likes she can come back with me for another year here.

Now I don't think I have any more news. Fred sends his love to you all, he is very very busy. With my best love to you all and to all our kind friends.

From your loving daughter

Lizzie

Orton was clearly accustomed to running smoothly without Vaca Diez, as it had done often in the past when he was away, and on one occasion in 1895 when he had been injured by a bullet. Fred was now preparing to go on his first 'tour'. The deceased parrot of which Lizzie writes was probably a Mathys family one – at any rate not her own, which had been left with the Strakers.

We have been here 6 weeks now and have not been able to get the European mail in yet, so I hope to receive a budget when it does come. Whilst I am writing I have one of those very big parrots with the long tails on my shoulder. He does not belong to me, but he comes at 6 o'clock in the morning and stays all day; he then goes home to sleep on the roof of one of the houses. I have to keep kissing him, or he pulls my ears and hair. He is such a funny old thing, he likes to lie on his back and for me to tickle him. I was sorry to hear that yours was dead; I will try and get another for you.

Now to begin the news; my last from you was October 31st from Bib and Bert. You were all well and I am happy to say we are also. Next week Fred starts on a long journey of 2 months to visit the different estates. Mr and Mrs Arnold are going too (she won't let Mr A. go alone, Fred is wild) so I am going to stay in the other house with Mrs Arnold's sister as we shall be alone. Poor Mr Arnold is henpecked, he can go nowhere without his wife and on this journey she will be dreadfully in the way.

I have a very good friend here in the wife of the French cook, the one who had her baby in the canoe on the road. She is so good to me, she makes my dresses and together we have made my rooms look quite pretty. I paid a visit to the carpenter's shop and got them to make an arrangement for my dresses and also a few tables which I have converted into washstands, etc. all with pale blue hangings. I have found out it is no use asking other people to get things done for you in this country, so I must march off myself to the workpeople and get everything done quickly. I should like Dad to see the different woods here, they make all the commonest things of most lovely cedar and then there is a red wood which would make beautiful furniture; they use it for burning in the launches.

The husband of the French lady (she is not a lady exactly, but I can't call her a woman either) has taken over all the eating arrangements and we live quite splendidly now. They are going to try and grow vegetables here, but it is very difficult on account of the insects. I have a grape vine at the back of the house and in one night the ants took all the leaves off; the fresh leaves come on again in a week and last night they took those off. I have an orange and lemon trees also, but no flowers. I am begging of the people of the launches to bring me roots and seeds from the different places. Fred does not start on his long journey for another fortnight, he will have to travel about a lot.

The ants which Lizzie accused of taking the leaves from her vine may have been *saübas*, the Brazilian name for leaf-cutting ants, notorious for the speed with which they can defoliate an entire tree. *En route* to the huge subterranean colony each ant struggles with a fragment of leaf many times its own size.

I thought of asking Bib to come out at first but then I thought she would not like to leave all her friends etc. We are expecting the mail in today, no letters have arrived for 3 months. The days here are very short. The gents work very hard in the office, they want more people here badly; they work Sunday morning as well. I am afraid my letters will get very dull. Every day is the same here, people come and go, it is very seldom that we are alone.

When I have had a rest of 6 months or so I shall take short journeys with Fred to see a bit of the country, but at present I have had enough of travelling.

All the entertaining, which as a manager's wife was obligatory, was not cheap and she had to count the pennies. 'Everything is so expensive,' she said. 'Champagne which is cheap stuff costs 24/– a bottle now. Think of it, a fourpenny bottle of ale is now 14/–, terrible.' Such prices cannot be translated simply, though to give an idea ale in Orton cost forty-two times its contemporary price in a public house in Hackney. But like everything else in Orton, the economics were simple. Rubber was inexpensive to produce and the rapids downriver kept import prices high. Coronel Labre had taken thirty-five days to get up the Madeira Falls, of which eight days had been spent passing just one set of rapids. His boats were dragged through the forest on wooden rollers. The price varied between 35s 6d and 52s 4d for every *arroba* of cargo – about 25 lb. These costs were added to the already high prices charged by the company store. Lizzie described to her family the kind of exploitation of the workers that was commonplace:

That is how they make such a lot of money over the rubber business. All the women, boys, and men have to go into the plantation and work alone; each has so many trees to tap and they don't grow together, sometimes a quarter of a mile between each tree. They make cuts in the trees and put a little basin underneath and a sort of milk runs out, and then they have to make a fire of a certain kind of nut, sit for days over this fire preparing the rubber milk. It is terrible work and more so when you know the prices they have to pay for their food, which consists of dried meat and rice and, alone in the forest for months, I should go mad. A lot of them die of consumption for the want of proper nourishment. I think I told you the children here sometimes take to eating earth. Well, I have a little savage girl of about 4 years, who eats her clothes. She only wears a little yoke dress, but in one night she has eaten great pieces of it. She tells the biggest lies and the only thing she is frightened of is a beating.

Please tell Bert to send more photographs, it is almost like seeing one of you to receive a photo.

Lizzie possessed the remarkable ability to comment with a certain dismay on what must, presumably, to her eyes have been remarkable scenes, but without being involved emotionally. She also appeared to forget Suárez. After leaving them behind in Riberalta, he was never mentioned again. Lizzie must surely have heard the *barraca* gossip, but possibly Fred told her not to write about it.

Nicholás Suárez was in fact not far downriver, two days at the most, and commanding a strategic point. Twelve and a half miles before the Beni enters the Madeira, it plunges in shallow falls over a rocky shelf. Navigation is impossible. Exploring the Beni in 1881, Suárez almost lost his life in these falls when his canoe overturned. According to family stories, Nicholás pulled himself ashore and knew instinctively that he had found the place for his *barraca*. By controlling the portage around the falls he was assured a levy on every *bolacha* of rubber sent downriver and a percentage of all goods ferried up from the Madeira. Family or not, it made no difference in business, so every bottle of ale downed by the staff at Orton added to Don Nicholás' fortune. Right at the start Suárez named the cataract the Falls of Hope – Cachuela Esperanza. Not content with controlling one portage, Suárez stationed his brother Gregorio at the Madeira–Mamoré Falls to take charge of cargo sent from London by their elder brother Francisco. The fourth brother, Romuló, was sent to Brazil, first to San Antonio on the Madeira, then to Manaus and Pará, to create a separate company for handling Suárez transactions on the main Amazon.

Every move in the expansion was masterminded by Nicholás, who maintained his firm control over the operation from Cachuela Esperanza; the headquarters flourished and so did Suárez Hermanos & Co. At Cachuela, the construction of offices and warehouses went on non-stop and ultimately Suárez built a short length of railway track to bypass the roaring *cachuela* of white water outside his front door.

Lizzie must have heard about Suárez' successes, even if only through the complaints of the clerks as the price of beer went up again. But her letters continue with no mention of him:

I wish you could see me now, I am sitting on the balcony writing and facing the river, my monkey is cuddling up to my 'boomdeay' [behind]. I have a parrot on each side and my dog is under the table.

And so life at Orton went on through the first year, and Lizzie's thoughts were fixed firmly on home. The 'Harmsworth' she refers to below meant one of the magazines published by the well-known newspaper proprietor Alfred Harmsworth, later Lord Northcliffe. *Home Chat* was also a magazine.

[Orton]
5 March 1898

My dear Bib,

Just a few lines to thank you for your letter and book ('Harmsworth') although you don't deserve a letter, you have not given me any news whatsoever. I always look forward to your letters to cheer me up, but this time I couldn't get up even the ghost of a smile. I suppose we are getting old, but I don't feel it. I even feel younger than ever although I have several white hairs.

You seem to be very gay with your parties and dances, I hope you manage to go a little bit swell. Louie seems to have grown a nice girl by her photograph; she seems to have the same character as I, and I only hope she will find someone to understand her as I have, otherwise she will not be happy. I must say that in these two years I have been happier in one way than ever, one must see a bit of the world to know how to live.

I am glad Lottie's children have turned out nicely, they must be a comfort to Dad. I am going to bring back a little savage as I can't bring a grandchild. Has Jack no idea of settling down yet? Don't you know of anyone very good and nice for him, he deserves to have a happy future, poor old Jack.

Why doesn't Rosie write to me? I am glad she visits Mrs Limberger now and again. I haven't received the *Home Chat* which Rosie promised to send me. I hope you have a bike by this time; I have not received mine yet, but I have a dear little horse and enjoy riding immensely. I am A1 at it now.

My family has decreased. It is minus the pig, poor thing, he used to go off to sleep in the pond and then when I had visitors return to the drawing room in such a sweet condition. I sent him off to heaven as I thought, but I don't know if he will get there, and I hear some wicked persons ate him.

My squirrel has gone off to the forest too, also one of my monkeys has died.

You would laugh if you could see Lizzie now. I have a little savage Indian girl to play the musical box whilst I write and she dare not leave off until I tell her, what I have learned in these parts you won't know me when I come back.

Who knows when I shall come back. I have forgotten what London is like. I shall be frightened to walk out alone; even in these parts to go to the next hut you must always take a servant.

Now, my dear girl, write to me often, cheer up, dance, etc. etc. etc.

With love from us both to all,

Your loving sister,

Lizzie

Dear Bib,

With best love to you and Rosie and kindest regards to Ben and Sonnie.

Yours Fred

Don't be afraid of writing to me one day when you feel like it and have nothing better to do.

Orton at first presented a gossipy, exciting social environment, but it did not last. In her letter dated 12 July 1898 Lizzie lost confidence for a moment; it was the first hint of trouble. Following the deaths of Vaca Diez in Peru and Francisco Suárez in London, Orton had become prime territory for a takeover. Shareholders had little chance to object to any deal in the Beni. She wrote:

The telegram has not arrived yet but we hear that the son of Vaca Diez is on his way out, so we do not know what will be our fate. At any rate we have saved enough money for Fred to start for himself in London if we do return this year.

Vaca Diez, careful to the last, had insured himself for £10,000 in London with the New York Equitable Life Assurance Co. The policy had been left in the care of Francisco Suárez. Vaca Diez had also made a will: the commercial house at Orton was not to be liquidated 'until the attainment of age by my son José Oswaldo who will take charge of the business . . .'. As executors, Vaca Diez appointed his brother Dr Hernando Vaca Diez and his cousin Nicholás Suárez. In a codicil, Vaca Diez 'required that Mr Bruno Arnauld should continue in charge of the management and administration until the year one thousand nine hundred in which his contract will terminate'. Mr Arnold, at least, was secure for another year.

Chapter Eight

'Never drink beer after reaching Buenos Ayres'

Before Fred set out to tour the outlying *barracas* they were expecting information from London, and Lizzie wrote home:

> We are anxiously waiting for the telegram from the Company to know if we are to stay here. I should not be sorry if we had to come home, sometimes I am very homesick . . .

Who would feel otherwise, with such a tangled web of affairs and so much uncertainty?

Settling Vaca Diez' estate was a laborious and complex process, expensive in terms of both time and money. The original will, in German and Spanish, had been drawn up in Trinidad, provincial capital of the Beni region of Bolivia; the codicil had been written at the Orton *barraca* in the year before Vaca Diez set out to raise capital in Europe. The folded document had been sewn shut with white thread; sealing wax had then been applied and marked with a coin of the national currency, 'owing to my not having the special seal', or so the regional public notary, F. Aurelio Paz, wrote on the cover. This alternative was legal in Bolivia, where Vaca Diez owned property.

When Lizzie first began to worry it was because the financial affairs of the company were run from an office in George Street in the City of London, and while on paper the company had £340,000 capital, Francisco Suárez, who had held power of attorney for Vaca Diez, was dead. The principal shareholders still alive were French bankers. Señora Lastenia Vaca Diez did not own shares, and under Bolivian law was entitled to very little; the six children were the sole heirs.

In Bolivia, Nicholás Suárez and Dr Hernando were executors, but their hands were tied since Vaca Diez had instructed that his business house, known as 'A. Vaca Diez' and which included the Orton *barraca*, should continue trading in its own right. And what the Beni lacked in law and order was made up for in bureaucracy. A paper mountain of stamped documents is a national goal throughout South America, and has been since the days when copies had to be filed back in Europe. So the rights of each beneficiary in Vaca Diez' will could not be verified quickly. Lawyers were paid for their time as well as their services, so they had no reason to rush. Even Nicholás Suárez, who wanted to get his hands on the rubber, could see that he would eventually be offered a bargain; he was prepared to wait.

Uppermost in Lizzie's mind, though, was Bert. As an engineer, Bert could get a job in Orton and be a companion for her. Lizzie's letter continued:

Now I am going to ask a great thing of you. Supposing the Company goes on and we stay here for another 3 years, we shall ask Bert to come out. But would you let Nell come with him; we would pay all expenses and outfit and Fred would meet them where they leave the steamer from Liverpool, i.e. in Manaos about October/November. It would not be a journey like we have made, but a perfectly safe one. I must have someone here and I think for Nell it would be very good. She must bring her books and music and I will educate her, do let her come. This is not the sort of life to suit Louie or I would have asked her, but there are too many people here to entertain and she does not care for that sort of life. Please let Nell come. Will write full particulars next mail.

Must finish in a hurry, with love from us both to all.

Your loving daughter,

Lizzie

Bert's expenses etc. would, of course, be paid by the Company. I will write fully when I get the Company's answer if they take the business or not. My brother Charles and his wife would come out at the same time and probably one or two more.

Yours Fred

[Orton]
27 April 1898

My dear People,

I wrote my last letter in a hurry as I did not know there was a launch going off, so I shall start where I left off in that letter. I asked you to let Nell come with Bert. If I could have her as a companion we should have a very decent life here, the climate is not at all bad, at present we are having some lovely breezy weather. We should have nothing to do but amuse ourselves and look after our clothes. I have already taken lessons in horse riding, but I do not like to take rides alone and the others don't care much about such things. Do let her come. I will take great care of her and we will come back together in 3 years time.

Lizzie yearned for her family to share the rubber profits even if they were destined to be short-lived. Perhaps, even more, she wanted one of her family beside her, and clearly Fred was considerate. As Lizzie had said in an earlier letter, she could not 'take home a grandchild'. The reason was never discussed at the time and later the Hessel family came to the conclusion that Fred was sterile.

The contents of the previous letter, which had been written in such haste, had obviously slipped Lizzie's mind, for she repeats many of its points here. Or maybe she was hoping that by repetition her arguments would become more persuasive. She is certainly most eager that Bert and Nell should join her.

Tell Bert I am awfully pleased that he still cares to come. We shall do our utmost to get him here, but we are not yet sure of the Company: his passage would be free and Fred would advance money for his outfit which would cost quite £25. But then he would have no expenses here and could soon settle that. The life here is a trifle disappointing and the clerks have to work hard, but still they have part of Sunday and above all can save a little money. And if Nell could come too we could have some nice family evenings. If he has time to study Spanish it would be good, but every language is useful abroad. In fact you can't know too much and above all to get along you must have confidence in yourself, commonly speaking, a little bit of cheek. I wish all the lot of you could come. It is very possible that Carl and Florrie Hessel will come at the same time as Bert and Nell. Fred wants Carl to manage the farming part of another estate 3 hours off from here. The Indians here are awfully queer people, they will come and sit outside your room and stare at you for hours. This morning I had 2 in my bedroom, they brought a dog with them too. Fred was still in bed under the mosquito net, I was in my nightdress. There they sat and I was waiting to take my bath. They don't like you to turn them away, but I did. I was not going to take my bath in front of them and with such a grand figure too. I told them to come back later on; it was 6 in the morning, if you please. They admire my clothes and my only beauty, my hair, too. They are struck with my nose, also, but I don't know whether with admiration or what. I haven't made it out yet.

Now goodbye, my dear people. One third of the second year has passed, we count the months to the end of our contract; but we don't want to come home until we have saved a little money, the life here spoils you for an economical one at home.

Please give my love and Fred's to all kind friends interested in us.

The bothering old parrot is on my shoulder, biting my ears and talking to me the whole time I write, I have to shut my doors to keep him out.

    With best love from us both,

    Your loving daughter,

    Lizzie.

I went riding yesterday and can hardly sit down today!

    Did Jack receive my note? Love to all, Fred.

If Fred wanted to establish himself at Orton he would need trustworthy people about him, such as his thirty-year-old brother Carl. Jack was the oldest Mathys son; he was running his father's business as John Mathys was in poor health. For the rest of the year, Lizzie learnt to live with uncertainty. She wrote early in each month to catch the downriver mail, and plans for Bert's visit progressed slowly.

To boost Lizzie's morale, the family sent books and magazines, but many were lost on the falls and she came to rely on the 'English gent in the next estate'. She read *Cassell's*, a monthly illustrated family magazine with plenty of fiction, price 7d. *Good Words* at 6d, another monthly, serialised novels and contained essays and travel articles, while the *Sketch* dealt with art and current affairs. Edna Lyall was the pen name of Ada Ellen Bayly, an immensely popular novelist of the period. Fashion was as thriving then as now, and Lizzie received her patterns from several magazines: *Fashion Illustrated* was a favourite, as were *Fashion of Today* and *Fashion and Fancies*; the newest one was *Fashion and Patterns*, first published in 1898.

The national dance of which she writes was probably the *cueca*, the best-known of them; it is not unlike some Scottish dances. The 'grandfather parrot' must have been a blue and yellow macaw, common in that part of Bolivia.

Orton, Bolivia

11 June 1898

My dear Dad and Mama,

    Since writing to you last I have received some letters, a lovely long one from Mama dated January 23rd, a fashion book and 2 magazines, also 2 letters from Alice and a fashion book. I was happy to hear, I can tell you. Fred has been away for 3 weeks, he came back last Saturday and in a few days is going off again for 2 months. We are both well. I have had a bilious attack now and again when we have been extra gay. This last week we had a Government gent here with his suite and soldiers, so we have been dancing, etc. I am going to learn the national dance to show you when I come back.

I have a tremendous family now, the people are beginning to know me and bring me things. This morning a gent brought me one of those tremendous grand-father parrots, he was shot in the wing and recovered; he is dark blue with a yellow breast and such a face, but he is such a dear old thing. Then I have the other red one and my monkey, which is quite tame now, a green parrot and my dog; also various little birds which came to be fed on the balcony, so I have enough to do, to feed and look after them.

Then the people bring me flowers, so I have something to look forward to when the launches come.

There is nothing fresh here to tell you, but when Fred comes back from this journey I am going with him to the other rivers for a 3 months' journey, partly by land, so I shall have something more to tell you. You say in your letter that Ben heard we had arrived in Orton, who told him that? It could not have been me, but I am glad for your sakes, it must have been a weight off your minds to know that we were safe. We have been here 3 months now and I have quite forgotten all our troubles and trials and feel like taking another trip, but this time we shall travel comfortably with our own servants and Indians, also plenty to eat and drink.

When you talk about the winter, I feel as if I don't want to come home again. Here we always have the sun, although it is a rather glaring one, and the moonlight nights are simply grand, one can easily read without a candle.

I am glad Jack has had a fairly good year, I suppose he has enough to worry him now he has the business all to himself.

So poor old Fred has gone back to Mexico, you must tell him all our news, I don't think letters from here would reach him, the service is so bad. At present do not send any books except the magazines, because they would get stolen, but we are going to make an arrangement with Pará to have all our letters and books sent on as cargo, then they arrive safely. I have several magazines sent regularly from an English gent in the next estate. *The Sketch, Windsor, St James Gazette*, also several comic papers from the engineers here, so I am not badly off. When everything is arranged I would like some good books sent out, one gets tired of the short magazine stories. *Good Words* is not at all bad, I like the story by Edna Lyall, also *Cassell's* I like very much. When I have finished with them I send them on to the next estate.

I am glad the girls are not yet tired of their piano. Tell Nell to practise a lot, that is the way to get on quickly.

How I do long to see you all. Wouldn't I love to come and have tea and bread and butter in the kitchen; I am so tired of the salt conserve butter, and the bread is horrid, they put heaps of lard in it and the flour is bad too.

Nearly half of the second year has gone, and I think we can say 1900 for our holiday. It is not so very far off, is it? What a time we will have and what a feed of lamb and green peas and cherries and strawberries. Fred sends his love to all of you, he will try and get a nice green parrot for Dad. What a pity your lovely one died, did it catch cold?

Now goodbye, all of you, with best love and many kisses from,
Your loving daughter, Lizzie
Please forward all letters and papers to Messrs Kanthack & Co. (for Mrs Hessel – Orton), Pará, Brazil.
They will pack everything in a box and then we shall get them safely.
With love to all, Fred

In late June 1898 Fred set out on his journey. The Orton holdings were mostly on the Orton River, within a few days of the *barraca*. Other company *estradas* were on the Tahuamanu River, a major tributary of the Orton. That part of the estate would take up to ten days to tour, and then they had 500 *estradas* on the Beni itself. Fred was away for two months, presumably checking the books at the local stores and buying rubber from smaller, privately owned *barracas*. A two-month journey could have taken him up the Orton River and into the Tahuamanu to a *barraca* known as Porvenir (a place with prospects), then overland on a short trail to a wretched conglomeration of shacks called Bahia, now Cobija, on the Acre River. This route had potential. The Acre River flows to the Purus and so to the main Amazon, also bypassing the Madeira Falls. One grandiose plan at the time envisaged a canal connecting the Acre to the Tahuamanu.

Orton, Bolivia
12 July 1898

My dear Mama and everybody,

It is ages since I received any news from you. An accident happened to our launch and we could not send down for the letters, but we are sending down boats tomorrow. I have been alone for 3 weeks now, Fred has gone on his long journey. I have had several letters from him brought by people when he passed on the road and so far he has been very unfortunate. The first day they lost one of the boats and the next had a slight accident with the launch, so he went on in a boat with his man and two gents who are making the journey with him, thinking it both safer and quicker. He sent me also a large bird from the mountains (Trumpetario).

Lizzie meant a *trompetero* or trumpeter, a handsome, purplish-black bird almost 2 feet high. Trumpeters keep mainly to the ground and are common pets in Amazon villages, as they have a reputation for killing snakes.

It is so tame and so pretty and every hour it makes a noise like a trumpet (don't laugh), not from its throat but from behind (a fact), a noise like a pigeon three times and then all down the scale like a trumpet very softly. I don't think there are any in the zoo. I shall try to bring a pair home with me. I had the blues most fearfully the first week alone, but now I am used to it. The French woman broke her arm, so I go to wash and dress her baby and then I take my meals at the other house and go for long walks in the forest with Mrs Arnold, always with 2 Indians carrying something to drink, and I have 2 Indian girls to sleep in my room. Fred is going to try and buy a little savage girl for me, they make splendid servants and here it is the custom to take one always with you, even if you only walk to the next house. They are a lot of trouble at first, but as a rule they learn quickly and are very faithful. For a little girl of 10 or 12 he will have to pay about £10, boys cost more.

My trumpeter has gone for a walk, but I do wish I had Nell here. I do want someone who loves me, these people here are so cold and gossip so dreadfully.

When Fred comes back he is going to have a little house built with a nice garden all to ourselves, so that we are not obliged to go out for our meals; the French woman wants to be our cook, with two Indians we shall like the life ever so much better if we are our own masters.

An English gent a little way off, knowing that I was alone, sent me up a lot of good English novels, wasn't it kind? Amongst them *The Mighty Atom* by Marie Corelli. Have you read it? An awfully nice book; all of them are good novels. I have no letters of yours to answer this time, but how I am longing for them.

I wonder if any of you are off for a holiday; if we come back rich we will take a house at the seaside for a couple of months for all of us. How grand to think of how we would enjoy ourselves.

Have you any news of Fred [Lizzie's brother] and Lottie? Tell Bib to write to me one of her letters as quickly as possible. When is she to be married? Why doesn't Louie write sometimes, I haven't had one letter from her. Tell her to send me in every letter a few flower seeds to put in my garden, she has more time than the others to collect them. How is Dad and how did he get on through the winter? I wish he could come here where it is always warm, he would get rid of his cough then.

For much of the year this part of the Amazon is tropically warm: the seasons are determined by the rains, which arrive in December and last for three or four months. Other changes come with the high water on the river, then again with low water and the appearance of the insect plague. Throughout the year the forest is green; there are no autumnal tints, and leaf fall continues all year round. Lizzie's 'winter' in July would have been characterised by a cold wind, overcast sky and chilling rain. In Bolivia the phenomenon is known as the *sur* or *surussu*: the temperature drops by 20–30 degrees Fahrenheit as air from the frozen pampas in southern Argentina reaches the Amazon. One *surussu* follows another from June to August, and it is not uncommon for the forest to be lashed by storms that each last a week. The best part of a *sur* is the fine, clear sky after it has passed.

We had our winter last week, 3 days of awfully cold weather. I shivered the whole time and no Fred to keep me warm. I shut all the doors and windows and put on my winter clothes. Poor Fred must have suffered camping out, although he has a good tent and two good rugs.

I had some more curios given to me, tigers teeth, monkeys teeth and feathers of the toucan and garça; we shot a lovely garça on the top of the house, they have never known a garça to come where there are people before, I think it must have been hurt. It had most lovely feathers, I have some of them, pure white.

I am longing to get Bert out here, perhaps I shall go with Fred to meet him at Manaos. I won't be left alone again. I should have been awfully wretched without the French woman, she is such a motherly sort, she knows what is the matter and what to do without asking. I couldn't go with Fred this time because there is no road, they have to make one and it is too rough for me, but he wants me to visit all the cattle places with him, which will take 3 months and most of the time on mules. I shall love it, we shall be free and no bothering señoras to think about.

Don't think I am grumbling, I am a bit homesick that is all, and I don't like the ladies here. I hate gossip and they have nothing to talk about, so they gossip fearfully.

Now, with love and kisses to all of you, write to me often one or the other, but I always look for Mum's letters first. From your loving daughter,

Lizzie

Tell Lou not to forget the flower seeds, I want to have the same flowers as you have.

Feathers from my trumpeter.

Orton, Bolivia
2 September 1898

My dear Dad and Mama,

I think it is more than a month since I have written to you, but never get anxious, the mails here are very irregular and there are also many letters lost over the waterfalls. So when you do not hear from us for a long time do not worry yourselves, we are very well here and the hot climate does not seem to do us any harm.

Fred has returned, I am glad to say, after being away for 2 months. I did miss him, I never passed such a horrid time in all my life I think. I did not sleep alone though, I had 3 Indians girls to sleep with me at first, but they gave me such a lot of trouble; one night they nearly set the house on fire, so I would not have them any more. The French woman came to sleep with me afterwards.

Fred did not have a nice journey, the river being very low. The second or third day they lost one of the boats and soon afterwards had an accident to the launch. And then with his land journey, he suffered very much, having to cross rivers on mule back, he was very often wet to the waist, but he has come back safe and sound I am glad to say. I wish you could have seen him when he arrived here, you would not have known him for the Fred of London! He came back like a brigand chief, a slouch hat, top boots, gun, etc.

Whilst he was away I went for long walks in the forest with Mrs Arnold, and I think I know Orton thoroughly now, but it is not exactly pleasant to take walks here. The heat is terrible and then there are so many flies, I always come back done for. I have nothing new to tell you of our life here, when people arrive we dance, play cards, etc., but when we are alone we go to bed at 8 o'clock. I think for 5 weeks or more I did not receive news from you, but a few days ago I received one letter from Bib and one from Nell. What is the matter with Bib to write such a serious letter, is it because she is engaged? I was quite disappointed, I always look forward to her letters to cheer me up. The letters were dated 18th March and I received them in August here. Isn't it a dreadful long time? I am always longing for news of you and the letters are always such a long time coming that I have the blues now and again.

Now for Bib's letter. If you received 3 letters by one post you must have been a very long time without news, but these must have been the letters which we gave to the Indians to carry, they always take longer, because in these out of the way places they do not send special canoes with the letters, they have to wait until they send their rubber down. It is true we had a dreadful journey, but it is not exciting, as Bib says, when you are hungry, you only think of your stomach and not of the lovely scenery, savages, etc.

Bib was very gay this last season with all her balls and actually Bert going in for dancing, I was very pleased to hear it, make him keep it up. I wish it was not such a difficult journey to get here, I would have Bib here for a few months, she would never find home dull any more; we never know when we are well off in this world. I am expecting a letter from Dad now, you must have known for some time that we arrived here safely and he said he would write.

Fancy Jack actually having a gas stove, what are the Mathyses coming to. I shan't know where I am when I come back, that is certain; but why don't you all vote for moving to a nicer cleaner place and not spend money on those tiny rooms? I don't know how Mum managed to get us all in, I am sure, you will have to put us up in a big tent in the garden, I am sure I cannot live in small rooms again.

Don't get wild with Lou when she is obstinate, I can sympathise with her, I used to be an awful mule; and poor Alice, how I used to aggravate her, we often laughed about it afterwards, she was always so fiery. I am glad Nell is progressing with the piano. Make her practise a lot and let her learn to sing also, even if she has not a good voice; one can always learn to sing one or two nice little songs.

Tell Bib to make a sketch of her intended, it is no use sending photos, the people steal them to decorate their rooms.

Who is the gentleman? What is he, why and wherefor? Tell me all about it please, is it finally settled? If it is, we hope they will be very happy.

Tell Nell I was very pleased with her account of Xmas and what a lovely birthday she had, too. Where has she managed to put all her nice presents? Has she won the bicycle in the competition of *Little Folks*? I wish I had left my bike at home with you girls, it is still spoiling in Iquitos. My family has increased considerably.

Fred brought some animals from the River Orton. I have now 3 trumpeters, 14 fowls, 2 green parrots, 3 big arara [the local name for a macaw], a kitten, a monkey, a small bird and 2 dogs, so now I am happy, but they give me plenty of work to feed them and keep them clean.

Fred has not received his telegram from the Company yet, but Mrs Vaca Diez writes that she thinks of coming with all her family, we do not know how things will go, but if we stay here, Fred means to have a nice little house, built all for ourselves. I get so tired of these Indians, whilst you are with them they work well, but as soon as you turn your back they do nothing and steal whatever they can.

I don't think I have any more news for you. Give my love to all please, Fred and Lottie, Carrie and all the friends of the family. I am always longing for news of you, so write as often as you can. Fred sends love to you all,

From your loving daughter

Lizzie

Kindest regards to all. I will write to Nellie by same mail, if I possibly can. Fred

Orton, Bolivia

3 October 1898

My dear Mama,

As I think you will receive this just about Xmas week, I will wish you all first and foremost a very happy Xmas and a prosperous New Year. I wish we were coming home to spend it with you, wouldn't I like a nice slice of turkey. We mean to have a nice Xmas here too, if we can possibly manage it. Mrs Arnold and I have settled on a tree which is growing in the forest close by, and every week we go to see if the tigers have eaten it.

Both Fred and I are very well and they say we are getting fat. It must be because we are lazy, it is not on the good things we eat.

I hope you are all well. I wonder what sort of winter Dad will have to get through; when I come back rich I will always take him to a nice warm place for the winter. I am sure I shall not be able to stand the cold weather any more.

I don't know whether I told you in my last letter that my latest child is a baby wild pig, he is such a dear little thing, follows me about like a dog, he goes out walking with me, always following close to my heels, much to the amusement of everyone. I wonder what I shall have next.

We have been very quiet for the last few weeks, nothing has happened at all; but we think of riding to the next village in a few days time, the Indians have just cut a road, a 6 hours ride; they are taming the mules for us now, they are all wild except two. It is like Buffalo Bill's show to see the men riding. I don't know how they manage to stick on. I can ride very well now and am not a bit nervous.

Buffalo Bill Cody's *Wild West Exhibition* had been staged at Earls Court in the week that Lizzie and Fred were married.

Fred has not received the telegram from the Company yet, so Bert must have a little more patience; as soon as things are settled they will send for several people to come out as clerks, warehousemen, etc. There are not nearly enough people here.

Yesterday all the Indians got drunk, it was a feast day, then they dance, sing and drink and sometimes fight, all day and all night; there is nothing they enjoy more than drinking and such horrid strong alcohol they drink, they will do anything for you for a bottle of it.

I received 4 books from you (*Cassell's*) a few days ago, but no letters, we expect them every day. I have now the whole take of Edna Lyall. I have also 4 good novels lent to me, one is *The Beautiful White Devil* – have you read it – a very nice book.

How I do wonder when we shall be coming home, how we shall find you all and if we shall have changed at all. I am afraid I shall get old quickly in this hot climate. I suppose there will have been a good many marriages and perhaps new families by that time. If Bert comes out I shall expect him to bring good and new photos of everyone. Dad as well, mind. It is no use sending them by post.

I have nothing more to tell you now, but I am longing to hear from you again. With best love from Fred and myself to everyone,

Your loving daughter,

Lizzie

They call me Dona Isabelita here, Spanish for Elizabeth [the diminutive, 'Little Elizabeth', a form of endearment].

A merry Xmas to you all, Fred.

Orton, Bolivia
6 November 1898

My dear Mama and everybody,

I was delighted to receive two letters from you last week, one from Bert dated 8th May, and one from you, May 22nd, also those lovely little photographs, they are splendid, every one of them,

and I do hope Bert will keep it up and send me some more.
The Mathys family albums contain the photographs of his grandmother at her table in 83 De Beauvoir Road, together with the pictures of the girls in their costumes, as well as Jack with his 'trilbies' (feet).

The one with Mum writing at the table pleased me very much, it is an exact likeness, even to the old inkstand, tilted up for want of ink as was always the case. The one with Dad, Mum and the polly is good too. Jack's trilbies caused great amusement, at first we could not make out his position, we thought the cushion was his boomdeay [behind].

The girls in their costumes are very nice. Louie is quite a young lady now and Nellie is taller than ever, Rosie looks just the same, but Jackie has grown up; the others have not altered at all. Do please send me some more. Couldn't you take a family group, also Rosie and bike, etc. etc. etc.

I am glad you received my letter from Orton, now you will not feel anxious about us, as we are very comfortable. We are alone now for 2 months, as Mr and Mrs Arnold have gone travelling, and, wicked to say, we are enjoying our liberty a little bit. We go out riding every afternoon, I have a new saddle and a little white horse. He is very shy, but I can ride him well now, gallop, trot and everything. I am so pleased that I have learnt it.

I can't make out why we do not receive letters from other people. We only hear from you, not even Rosie now, and other friends never. I hope they are not tired of writing so soon.

I have received the 6 months *Cassell's*, all together and opened; I think someone on the road must have kept them to read and then sent them on afterwards. They are fearful people here in that way. Of *Good Words* I have only received 4, but the Xmas number I have, also the fashion books, thank you very much.

My English friend has also received a box of 30 good novels, he sent me some the other day. We spent 3 days in his village a week ago and had an awfully jolly time. There are about a dozen nice ladies there, so we danced, walked, champagne, etc. The change did me a lot of good.

It did not take Lizzie long to sum up the partnerships in Orton. Victorian Amazon travellers usually mentioned the 'loose morals' of the locals, and Lizzie in her own way was no exception. 'She is not a lady exactly, but I can't call her a woman either . . .' Talk of 'bush wives' may seem an old joke worn thin amongst foreigners staying for long overseas, yet taking a *compañera de cama* was the custom upriver. Sometimes the girls would be *mestizos*, of mixed Indian and European blood, though just as frequently the men would find an Indian partner, raise a family and settle there. The locals never even bothered to comment.

I had had the blues for a week, now I feel quite fresh again. I do not know of any particular paper that I should like, I am glad to receive all, but for patterns, only blouses, gowns and fancy collars will do here, if you happen to come across any.

The people here have been very excited about the war, but we only get scraps of news from one and the other.

This war was the bitterly fought Sudan campaign. By November Lizzie may just have received news of the Battle of Omdurman, fought on 2 September – though more likely she had been told about the Battle of Atbara River on 8 April. The British Army, under General Kitchener, in collaboration with Egyptian forces, had crushed 18,000 Mahdists, killing 5000 and taking 10,000 prisoners. A report of the war appeared in the *Gaceta del Norte*.

Tell Carrie I am looking forward to her letter. I promised to write to her mother, but I have not their address, please give my regards to her family. I wish I could have seen the bluebells and lillies in your garden, there are no flowers like the English, nor fruit either, how I do long for some cherries and green apples. We have plenty of melons and pineapples now, but there is no other fruit except oranges in this part of Bolivia.

I am glad you keep my letters, I shall like to read some of them over when I come back; we have already forgotten our troubles and hardships of that journey.

Towards the end of 1898, their second Christmas away from London, the precarious situation at Orton seemed to be improving. At last there seemed to be a chance that Bert could be found work and a passage to Bolivia.

Tell Bert I like his letters and am looking forward to some more. I hope he is keeping up his Spanish as there is still a chance. I am still a Mathys, I can't stick to my grammar, but I speak fairly well. Fred speaks perfectly and even writes for the newspaper sometimes in Spanish, but he has been through the grammar 3 times and has a good memory.

Tell them all to write to me. If they could only see in what a lonely spot we are and so far away from Europe they would have pity and write often, it is only the Mum who never forgets. We have been away nearly 2 years now and we are already talking of the good times we will have when we come back.

With best love to Dad, yourself, and the rest of the family, from Fred and myself,

Your loving daughter,

Lizzie

Love to all,

Fred

Orton, Bolivia
6 December 1898

My dear Mama,

I received a letter from you dated July 26th in which you say you received a surprise present. I am glad my letter arrived safely and that the money was paid; we have received news lately that our accounts have been paid, so that looks good for the future.

One of the sons of the late Vaca Diez has arrived from London. He is very nice to us and only associates with us at present; he says he has come to learn the business here, but of course has no power in it whatsoever. He is sure the Company is settled, but so far Fred has not received instructions from Europe; we both are longing to come home again, that I can tell you, although we have only been away 2 years.

I am glad you are enjoying your little bit of shopping. I only wish it had been a £50 note. How Rosie and I used to enjoy ourselves when we had a little bit of money to spend; well, I hope we shall have some good times together again. I am looking forward to the letters from the girls. I haven't received one from Louie yet, she must be Dad's secretary and write a special letter from the two of them. I thought of Dad on his birthday. I hope we shall have enough money to go to his old house during our first holiday.

I received your two *Quivers*, they are nice books. I always cut out the pictures, they are such good ones, and put them on my wall. I also received the paper books and think them very good.

Lizzie had obviously sent her mother some money to spend on herself. The *Quiver* was a Sunday magazine for general reading and cost 6d; published monthly by Cassell, its stated aims were the 'defence of biblical truth and the advancement of religion in the homes of the people'. Addie, mentioned below, was Addie Foot, Lizzie's cousin on her mother's side, and now living in New Zealand.

It is best not to send out anything in the way of lace, etc. I should never receive it, only what can be enclosed in letters.

I am glad Lotty arrived safely with her family, you have the house full again now. I am longing to see a nice English garden again, here the seeds from Europe won't grow, they come up too quickly and there are really no flowers worth mentioning.

When you write to Addie again tell her to enclose a note for me and I will do the same. I should like to hear of her life out there, I expect it is very different from ours. Here we have everything at our command and she seems to have to rough it. I expect it has done her good in one way, she was never very fond of work.

I suppose you heard all about Louie Hessel's wedding. We have now received news of the arrival of a son, and they have called him Fred.

Do you remember a Mrs Kaufman who came to see me once at 83, her husband was a friend of Fred's and went to Buenos Ayres, she joined him afterwards with her baby (my goddaughter). Well, Fred has received a letter from Mr Kaufman saying that his wife is dead and has left him with 3 little children. Isn't that sad? She was such a strong stout girl, I can hardly believe it. He is returning to London soon with his little family. It is a pity there are no trains in these parts, we are so very close to Buenos Ayres and yet it is a journey of 10 weeks from here.

There is nothing fresh in our life here, but I think there will be soon, with this young Vaca Diez and the Company settled; also Mrs Arnold thinks of leaving for a better climate, she is always ill, so I shall be the boss of the show.

Two other ladies have arrived here lately, but as is very common in these parts, they are not married, their so-called husbands are clerks in the house. One of them is not bad, but I can't make *friends* of them, or the people here would talk. In these small villages very few people are really married, perhaps a priest passes once in a year and then he has enough to do, it is nothing but baptising, marrying and feasting the whole time.

Give my love to Dad, sisters and brothers and friends and accept a lot for yourself.

From your loving daughter,

Lizzie

How I look forward to Mum's letters!

Orton, Bolivia
27 January 1899

My dear Mama,

Xmas has come and gone and we have now commenced our third year. Fred has written to Bert by this mail, I do hope he can make satisfactory arrangements with the Company and arrive here in July. The route he is coming by is a long one, but it is a safe one, and I am sure he is the one to enjoy the journey thoroughly; he will find in Mr Walton a good companion, too.

Fred is advancing the money for outfit, etc. He must be very careful not to get robbed on the way, there are always people about who try to take advantage of fresh arrivals and when he has settled down here he can pay Fred back by degrees; he won't have many expenses here as he will live with us and his outfit will last him 3 years, so he ought to be able to save at least two-thirds of his salary. Then when he is tired of this climate he will have a little capital to start wherever he likes, it seems to me worth trying. It will be a good medicine for us to see a face from home.

Fred sent a businesslike letter to Bert, who must have wondered how he could live on £120 a year if the price of ale was really as high as Lizzie said.

Orton, Bolivia
29 December 1898

My dear Bert,

Your letter without date, in which you tell me that you are still desirous of coming out to us, duly reached me at the time.

I am writing to the Secretary of the Orton (Bolivia) Rubber Co Ltd, 15/16 George Street, Mansion House, to engage you on a contract for 3 years after arrival here as general clerk, traveller and/or architect, at £120 for the first year, with free station, salary to be increased according to services. His name is Mr Phillips; if he is not there the Trustee, Mr Ries, will see you.

Money: If the contract is accepted, they will book your passage to Buenos Ayres and hand you £25 – for your journey from Buenos Ayres to Santa Cruz. From the latter place, or from Puerto Suárez you will be dispatched for account of the house, without any further expense to you.

They will also advance you £30 – towards your outfit. The enclosed list will serve you as a basis and I would only repeat that your 2 boxes or trunks must be strong and not larger than 31×18×13 inches – you must only bring the necessary for the journey and the beginning here, as it does not do to travel with a lot of luggage over so long a route.

Besides the above my cousin, Mr Limberger, will hand you £50 for my account, in gold, of which you may use whatever you want, but keeping a cashbook, so that we can adjust the account when you arrive here.

All your travelling expenses will be paid you by the firm here, also your passage home will be paid at the end of contract.

Please see that both my brother Charles and Mr A. Walton, who will be coming with you, keep strict accounts.

My brother's address you will obtain at Mr Limberger's 4a St Dunstan's Alley and Mr Walton's is c/o Heilbut Symons & Co. 34 Fenchurch Street.

Please communicate with them and settle everything for the best.

You will follow the instructions given on the enclosed list.

Bert was advised to book a passage by steamer to Buenos Aires calling at Bahia (now Salvador) and Rio de Janeiro in Brazil. From Buenos Aires he was to travel by riverboat up the River Plate and Paraguay River to Asunción, capital of the tiny, landlocked republic of Paraguay. The whole of that journey would take five or six weeks. At Asunción he would have to disembark and change to a smaller shallow-draught steamer, to take him upriver to Corumbá in Brazil. From Corumbá Bert had to cross the swamp-edged river to the mosquito-infested Puerto Suárez in Bolivia. With high water that part of the journey could take another two to three weeks; in low water it would be impossible. But this was the 'back door' route and, as Lizzie said, 'long but safe'.

As far as Puerto Suárez Bert was to expect just the usual river problems, but on the overland mule trek to Santa Cruz he could expect swamps, scrub jungle with rattlesnakes, 'savages' and broad rivers. The rivers, including the Rio Grande, he had to ford. The route had been opened up in 1880 by Miguel Suárez Arana, who had gained a government concession to forge a way to the Paraguay River.

Once in Santa Cruz Bert would have to travel another week on horseback to the headwaters of the Mamoré River; then after another month of boats and a few more hostile tribesmen he would get to Orton. All this effort was being made to avoid the Madeira Falls, the Isthmus of Fitzcarrald or the Purus River, increasingly under Brazilian control.

But Fred sensed that company affairs were going his way, and he needed help. The trading house of A. Vaca Diez could be his to run, and Mr Walton from the London office and Fred's brother Carl or Charles, who were supposed to be accompanying Bert, received similar instructions. He wrote to Bert:

Orton (Bolivia) Rubber Co. Ltd. I have not yet taken over the house A. Vaca Diez for the Coy, but have instructions to do so. Should the Secretary, for some reason or other, decline to make the contract you will please write to me at once and will make you another proposal for the end of the year – to come over the Acre river.

There is, however, not much doubt that my proposal will be accepted.

You will – if you are coming – go and see Mrs Lastenia Vaca Diez, 79 Priory Road, West Hampstead, and tell her that you are coming out to Orton. Ask her if she has any message for her son Oswald (who arrived here on the 1st inst) and give her my and Mrs Hessel's [Lizzie's] Kindest regards. She does not speak English, but her children do.

Tell her that Mr Oswald is in good health and looking after her interests, also that my brother Charles is coming out, but that he is in Portland or Woolwich, or wherever he may be, and that he may not have time to call on her.

I enclose copy of a letter to Mr Walton, which you will please post on to him, after reading it and making your notes.

I rely upon you to see that you travel in perfect understanding.

You will also go and see Mr Pedro Suárez of 12 Fenchurch Street and listen to any advice he may give you, as he knows these parts. When you see him say that you have come to see if he has any orders to give you for the Beni river. I am writing to him about you.

Do not postpone your departure beyond the 20th May or thereabouts from Southampton, as otherwise you will get into the rainy season, which will make your land-journey unpleasant. The 20th June will do, in case of need, but no later. Get a passport through Mr Limberger.

With kindest regards to all

Your affectionate brother

Fred

With the long lists of clothes and medicines, Fred enclosed a list of do's and don'ts.

GENERAL RULES TO BE OBSERVED

– Avoid sun, rain and nightdew.

– Avoid getting your feet wet.

– Do not bathe in the river.

– Do not waste your bullets.

– Do not go ashore in Bahia or Pernambuco; and in Rio de Janeiro only if there is no yellow fever about.

– Never drink too much.

– Do not trust strangers. Be civil to strangers but reserved, lend no money to anyone and do not trust to people who offer their services. Keep ½ money in a strong belt with pockets inside which you will wear always, the other ½ divide in your boxes, when going ashore take only little with you, leaving the rest of your belt money with the Captain or Steward (preferably before witnesses when not sure of latter).

– Take fruit salt 2 or 3 times a week.

– Eat *no fruit.*

– See that your bowels are open every day.

– In case of sickness, consult the people of the place, who generally know how to treat local complaints.

– When riding use *no* spurs, unless you are sure of yourself in the saddle. A stick or whip is good enough to make the animals go.

– *Arms*   A Winchester carbine 44 (12 shots) is necessary also a revolver with 100 bullets each. Keep them clean, in fact I should like you to keep all the weapons of your party in good order whilst travelling.

– In case of an attack by savages, between Puerto Suárez and Santa Cruz, seek shelter behind a tree and aim low in the chest or stomach as they have a way of dodging. Stand your ground and never show the white feather.

– The rifle is necessary as there are tigers and savages between Puerto Suárez and Santa Cruz. The savages hardly ever attack now, but it is as well to be prepared and camp in sheltered spots, when they can be found.

– Cold tea or cold coffee is better than water when you are thirsty.

– Never drink beer after reaching Buenos Ayres.

– If you get wet a little Cognac is all you want.

– A bottle of Glycerine is good to bring in case of thirst where no water is to be had.

– A hammock and mosquito net you will get in Puerto Suárez. Until then you will be on board the steamers where you have your berth. In Puerto Suárez (at Messrs Voss & Stoeffen) you will also get the necessary pots, pans, cups, spoons and forks, and a few conserves, if there are any. Dried meat and rice will be your chief food during the mule-journey. The drivers will do the cooking, saddle your horses, or mules, fix your hammocks & ca. If you can get tents or tarpaulins in Puerto Suárez, take them; even if they are only just large enough to cover your mosquito net ceilings, to keep off the dew, or rain. See that you are well covered during the night. The early mornings are fresh, and I expect you will even, in July, have a few cold days.

In a separate letter Lizzie added a few practical, sisterly thoughts:

. . . Of course there are a few odds and ends Fred has not put down, such as scissors, pocket knife, soap, tooth brushes, sponges, also a microscope, if you can afford it; camphor, and napthaline pack in your clothes. The girls must mark your clothes nicely.

You must bring photos of everyone for me.

Mind you buy your clothes in a good shop and all of good quality so that they last a long time. I have changed my mind about asking Nell to come with you; in the first place, the journey is too long and rough and then the heat I think she could not stand. The responsibility is too great, I should never forgive myself if anything happened to her. I hope she will not be disappointed, she shall be my companion during our first holiday.

With love and best wishes for your journey

Your loving sister

Lizzie

Bring as many flower and vegetable seeds as you can (in a small way) in soldered tin boxes. Mark your trunks (boxes) 'Transit – Bolivia'.

Chapter Nine

'One must think of health before wealth'

Lizzie enjoyed the Christmas of 1898, and wrote home:

> How did you pass your Xmas? I suppose Rosie was with you. We had a nice one; we got a large palm tree from the forest and I managed to secure a few small candles and odds and ends from a German House close by. We decorated it and it was splendid. Fred made a punch and we sat up, five of us, talking of home and drinking punch. New Year's Eve was also nice. We played cards until 12 o'clock, then we fired shots, put up the flags and rang all the bells (dinner and workmen's bells); it was quite exciting. Then we had something to eat and drank punch until 5 o'clock in the morning. I quite enjoyed it. All the Indians got mad drunk and enjoyed themselves too, that is their idea of a feast.
>
> I have neuralgia badly today . . . .

The New Year began with thoughts of her family. John Mathys was ill, and Lizzie did not know whether or not his condition was serious. She wrote to her brother Jack:

> This is a sort of confidential letter. I don't think we can return in under three years and I should like to know exactly how things are going on.

She was obviously concerned.

> Take great care of poor Dad until we return, when I hope we shall be able to take him to his old home. We have been thinking of it for a long time if only things go well; but there are so many risks with the climate etc.

For some time Lizzie had been writing her letters just to 'Dear Mama', and it seems that John Mathys' illness persisted throughout the year. Preparations for Bert's visit continued, and Fred wrote to his cousin, Mrs Limberger, who was given a shopping list for Lizzie. Bert was asked to pack everything with his tropical outfit, including some new photographs of the family.

> You must get Ben to take photos of you all or a family group. Do the girls know of one or two very pretty waltzes? Tell Nell to make me a very pretty pocket to hang on the wall of my sitting room to put photos in. I wish you could all pack yourselves into Bert's trunk.

January and February passed quickly in Orton; Fred was even more deeply involved with the company, and Lizzie still concerned about her piano. 'I have no piano at present, but it is on order and perhaps it will arrive in a year or two.' They had resigned themselves to staying in Orton on whatever terms they could get. The mail service never improved and letters often crossed in the post – sometimes by several months. Lizzie said, 'Such things as stamps we do not know here. All our letters are packed up and sent to Pará.' The delays were bad: 'I am happy to say that I have just received a whole parcel of letters and books from you dated from July to October,' – the previous year.

Bert had left for Europe, instead of coming to Bolivia, but Lizzie was not crushed by the news.

Of course I am sorry that Bert has decided not to come, but on the other hand I am pleased he is getting on well in Europe. I should not like him to give up a sure thing for a venture, and to be near you all is worth a great deal too.

The Hessels had been accepted warmheartedly into the local community in Orton, as Lizzie explained in her February letter.

I am about to be a godmother and Fred a godfather to an Indian child here; they think it such an honour to have their *patrón* as *compadre*, they call it. Of course, I have had to dress the child and mother for the occasion and we are going off to the next village this afternoon where there is a priest. . . .

We went to the baptism in the Catholic Church. I had to provide a white robe and a satin bonnet for the child.

The church is a small room arranged with an altar, nothing else, no seats whatsoever; everything passed off nicely. We stayed there 4 days, shopping, walking and dancing, but the floors are so bad for dancing that I hurt my foot and am losing the nail of my big toe. I must say I am one of the best dancers here and have to dance with 3 or 4 gents. I get very tired but there is no help for it.

Tomorrow it will be one year since we arrived here in Orton. I wonder how long it will be before we can come home. Fred has such a responsible position that I don't know how we shall be able to take a holiday unless one of the new clerks turns out extra special. But still we live in hopes of coming home in the year 1901; before I don't think it possible.

All these vignettes of *barraca* life never went beyond immediate, everyday affairs; yet the river 'telegraph' was filled with disturbing stories of problems in the Acre. The Acre was not just a river, it was also the name of a sprawling forest between the Acre and Purus Rivers. The extent of the Acre changed according to various opinions concerning the northwest boundary, and they hinged about the source of another river, the Javari. While this created a complex puzzle for geographers and politicians, a far more serious problem was developing as Brazilians moved upriver from the Amazon into the Acre. By far the largest number of settlers were the destitute and pathetic *flagelados* from the impoverished northeast. Crammed shoulder to shoulder on the steamers, these emaciated people moved in their thousands into the Amazon's richest rubber country.

By agreement the Acre was Bolivian, even though it was far more accessible to Brazil. Few Bolivians or their government ever reached the Acre, though eventually Brazilian penetration reached the attention of the authorities in the Beni. The Orton business was not directly involved with the boundary problem but was interested because of the potential for trade, and, as Vaca Diez had realised in Pará, there was a political time bomb on the doorstep. While Fred and Lizzie had been enjoying Christmas, the Bolivians were making obvious moves to open a Customs post at Puerto Alonso on the Acre River. It seemed a simple way to make money and fill the power vacuum at the same time – also the government presence would be self-financing: build a shack and raise the flag, then install a Customs officer with a rubber stamp to charge a tax on every *bolacha* sent out of the country and on any goods coming in.

The trees were of the finest quality and abundant, so nobody needed a Customs post – especially a Bolivian one. A highly charged 'Acre for the Acreanos' movement began to take shape: there were 60,000 Brazilians in the Acre, so the Customs post would not stand a chance.

To make matters worse, the Bolivians decided to impose a 30 per cent export tax. To the Acreanos this was the ultimate challenge and they decided to take the law into their own hands. In March 1899 the Puerto Alonso post was attacked, and as a result the free passage of Acre rubber, the freebooting way of life and the duty-free importation of ladies of pleasure and French perfume were assured. As glasses were raised in the Acre, the state of Amazonas applauded too; Acre rubber was taxed as an export from Manaus. Pará was less enthusiastic: *aviadores* from Pará were busy in the Acre and welcome among the Brazilians; Pará, if given the chance, would prefer 'foreign' control of the territory. Indeed, the Paraenses preferred the idea of the Acre under Bolivian control to that of it being a satellite of Amazonas.

While everyone outside the Acre was hearing news of the attack on the Customs post and trying to adjust to the situation, events in the heart of the forest moved quickly. Luis Galvéz Rodriguez, a Spanish colonist, born leader and inept politician, proclaimed independence unilaterally – the slogan 'Acre for the Acreanos' was chanted the length and breadth of the river, and on 14 July 1899 Luis Galvéz named himself President of the fledgeling republic of Acre. With a band of rubber tappers Galvéz took possession of the aggravating Customs post and raised the revolutionary flag, a yellow and green diagonal bearing a red star, embellished with the traditional cap of liberty, a shield, a laurel wreath and the date, '*14 de Julho 1899*'. Being remote from authority and with unchecked symptoms of megalomania, Galvéz proceeded to consolidate his gains. In Puerto Alonso, or Pôrto Acre as it was called, streets with Brazilian names such as Rua Brasil and Rua Ceará were laid out. The President renamed a run-down *barraca* the Galvéz Palace, mustered a band of stalwarts and set about drawing up a constitution and some sort of legal system. The motley cabinet first considered taxes. Any new republic has cash flow problems and Acre was no exception; on the other hand its Treasury had collateral. The Acreano 'Finance Minister' knew that three million lb (1350 metric tonnes) of rubber had passed down the Acre River in the first four months of that year. His idea was simple – to tax it. With his finance problems solved, the fact that he had alienated both Brazil and Bolivia did not concern Galvéz, and his government drew up maps presenting the boundaries of the new state.

However this show of defiance only a hundred miles or so from Orton failed to get even a passing mention from Lizzie, who from March onwards was mostly concerned with company affairs and a £200 draft, presumably a loan which Fred had promised to send to Jack. At last Lizzie and Fred seemed to be making enough money to enable them to be generous.

> Fred says he will write to you by next mail. He is to sign the transfer within 3 days, when he will arrange about the £200.00. He has met with a great many difficulties in taking over the Company, but we hope they are at an end now. He is liked by everyone in this part and I think with the Capital of the Company will be able to improve the business considerably. He wants to make enough money to return to Europe for good. Perhaps we shall stay a year over contract instead of taking a holiday; that is if we keep well, in this climate one must think of health before wealth.

Then in April came their first success, when, according to Lizzie, some of the Orton affairs were resolved. Fred was given authority at the

Above *In the late nineteenth century, many construction camps blossomed in the Amazon, as money flowed from Europe and America to fire the rubber boom*

Right *Indians of the upper reaches of some Peruvian Amazon tributaries wear cloak-like cushmas. These people were exploited during the rubber boom, being hunted in the forests by traders on 'slaving expeditions'*

Above *Iquitos 1897: Lizzie wrote on the back of the photograph that it was a 'Group taken in country. The fat one is Vaca Diez'*

Below *Iquitos 1897: the house of Mr Weiss. Lizzie with some of the clerks. Lizzie wrote on the back of the photograph, 'Taken in drawing room on my birthday'*

Above *Iquitos 1897: Lizzie with
the housekeeper and a number of the
clerks. She had written 'Dinner table of
Mr Weiss' on the back of the
photograph. Note the little 'savage' on
the far right of the picture*

Below *Lizzie's mother in the garden of
83 De Beauvoir Road. 'The photos
with Mum writing at the table pleased
me very much,' wrote Lizzie in a letter
dated November 1898*

Outfit for Orton (Bolivia).

	Valuation
1 dark grey or brown travelling suit	£ 3. -. -
2 light suits (jackets, no morning coats) thin stuff, no lining	. 6. -. -
2 grey Alpaca coats, or silk, no lining	. -.12. -
2 pairs flannel trousers, unshrinkable, serviceable color	. .1.10. -
1 pair cloth do. thin, but strong	. -.15.6
6 pants of thin unshrinkable wool, or gauze	.1.5. -
6 do. linen	. -.15. -
12 gauze vests	+ .12. -
5 flannel shirts with collars, as Mr Melchior sent them	
to me when in Pará (Newling 13/-)	. 5. 4. -
3 pyjama suits, thin flannel	. 1.17.6
4 body belts	. -.10. -
2 trouser .	. -.5. -
3 white linen shirts	. .1.1. -
12 collars preferably turned down	- .10. -
18 handkerchiefs ½. a dozen	- .13.6
12 ties	- . 12. -
10 pairs socks, merino or thin wool	-. 18. -
1 Macintosh, sewn, not gummed	1.10. -
3 pairs strong, handsewn lace-up boots	3. 3. -
1 pair leather leggings for riding	- .15. -
2 strawhats	- . 4. -
1 soft felt hat for travelling	- . 7.6
2 travelling caps	- . 3. -
1 muffler	- . 5.6
2 bath towels	- . 5. -
4 hand .	- . 4. -
1 Umbrella	- .12.6
a Spanish Grammar	-. 4. -
a few books to read on the road	-. 10. -
	£ 34. 4. -

Medicines

2 bottles of Eno's fruit salt	-. 4. -
2 small bottles of quinine pills (preferably Pelletier ∞ ½gr)	-. 2. -
(to be taken in case of fever: 4 evening, 2 morning)	
chlorodyne, 8 drops in a little water, for Diarrhoea	-. 1.6
a few boxes of opening medicine (Rhubarb pills)	-. 0.6
1 box of Witch hazel oil ⎰ for sore legs	
or vaseline ⎱ from riding	-. 1.6
1 pot of Vaseline	-. -.6
1 bot glycerine, a few drops taken to alleviate thirst	-. 1. -
1 bot ammoniac for insect bites	-. 1. -
cottonwool, linen, courtplaister	-. -
forward	£ 34. 17. -

Mr. A. Mathys.
Mr. A. Walton.

La casa de la Cia   The Orton Rubber Co.

Demmer Riberalta

Our invitation card for the ball on "Huascar"

James Good,

suplica á U.e se digne acompañarle á temar una taza de té. abordo del "Huáscar", á las 8 y media de la noche del Viérnes 19. invitación que se transferirá para el Sábado en caso de lluvia.

MARZO 17 DZ 1897.

Above 'Such a place is Orton,' Lizzie said after her long journey. This postcard of the grand house of Antonio Vaca Diez at Orton was brought to England by Major (later Lt-Col.) Percy H. Fawcett in 1907

Below An invitation card sent to Lizzie and Fred inviting them to a party on board the Huascar to celebrate the birthday of Captain Good. Translated into English the invitation reads 'James Good requests the pleasure for you to take tea aboard the Huascar at 8.30p.m. on Friday 19 March. In case of rain the invitation is changed to Saturday'

Above *After it was collected, the rubber was weighed and stored in warehouses, often in remote parts of the Amazon, before being shipped to Europe. Occasionally the rubber was adulterated to increase the weight; but dealers were always on the lookout as quality not quantity was the key to success*

Opposite above *A group of Indians and their overseer. The rubber forests of the Amazon were scoured by professional Indian hunters to round up the strongest men for work as tappers. The weaklings were beaten or killed*

Opposite below *Latex was turned into a solid mass by dripping it on to a pole which was rotated slowly in smoke which came from smouldering palm nuts. It was an unhealthy, poorly paid way to eke out survival in the Amazon. Many of these 'tappers' never returned to their homes*

Above *The milky latex from the Hevea or rubber trees was collected each day by seringueiros who usually worked alone in the forest*

Above *Roger Casement*

Left *Machiguenga Indian. Children were 'torn sobbing from their mothers' arms' – or so American engineer Walter Hardenburg revealed in his account of the Amazon. Three years earlier, in 1906, a Peruvian newspaper had drawn attention to the conditions on the Madre de Dios River*

barraca and took over the company, though Lizzie never explained the details. Her letters confirmed that a deal had been struck in Bolivia, presumably in Riberalta, the nearest 'official' town.

Orton, Bolivia
7 April [1899]

My dear Mama,

I have no news for you, but as there is a boat going down river I must let you know that we are alive and well. We passed our Easter very quietly, there were a few people here, but we did not get up a dance as there were no ladies. I am a bit tired of entertaining and shall be glad when we have a few days to ourselves.

The Company was finally settled on the 1st April, so now we are real bosses and can order about as we like. Everything was settled in the next village, where live the judge, lawyer, etc., and a ball was given in honour of the occasion. I could not go as my foot was not well enough; they think of giving a ball here in Orton too.

How are you all at home? I am longing to hear from you again and also I am looking forward to a few more photos. I wonder if Bert will make up his mind to come out after all.

I must hurry as the boat is going out soon; we never know exactly when we can write, the boats arrive unexpectedly, stop half an hour and off again.

We are still dressmaking, making a white sailor dress trimmed with pale blue. I set the fashions here; everyone copies my dresses. I have always to rack my brains for a new style because I like to be different to the others, so if you find anything original please send it.

Now goodbye, with love to you all and best wishes for your summer holidays,

From your loving daughter,

Lizzie

A month later Lizzie again wrote to Jack. It seems that the ideas that Fred had nurtured since his days in Bordeaux were paying dividends.

Orton, Bolivia
8 May 1899

My dear Jack,

Enclosed you have a copy of Fred's letter and draft, in case the first should get lost. If you would like to have another, say £500, Fred will only be too pleased to let you have it; you would then be able to work on a larger scale and get on the road to fortune.

We are going on in the same way and count that this month 2

129

years hence we shall be on our way to Europe with nice liver complaints. If Fred decides to make a fresh contract we may get home before. I am writing to Nell by this mail, so will keep all my news for her letter.

With love and best wishes for the future.

from your loving sister,

Lizzie

Fred says if you would like to send Dad to Switzerland with one of the boys or yourself or Mama, he would gladly take half of the expenses to his account. I shall send a copy of this letter by next mail in case this should get lost.

Life in Orton began once again to sparkle for Lizzie with the booming rubber trade and more visitors. But Lizzie still never mentioned the Acre, even though reports appeared in *La Gaceta del Norte*, one of them directly beneath a company announcement signed by Fred. The build-up to Galvéz' unilateral declaration of independence was creating concern along the Orton, particularly for the Suárez family. After the Acre, the Orton would be the next target for any expansionist policies and then would come the Beni. Nicholás Suárez had an answer: as the most powerful Bolivian influence in the area, he decided to build strong *barracas* along the unresolved frontier line. The line he chose for defence bore little relation to any boundary as drawn on maps, and tended to follow local trails and *estradas* in the deep forest.

As far as Lizzie was concerned Orton was the epitome of tranquillity, though this may only have been the impression she wished to convey. After all, her father was ill, Bert was not expected in Orton, and, as always, she was thinking of the fortunes of Rosie and Ben.

Fred was effectively the manager, and his name appears frequently in the *Gaceta*. At this time Lizzie mentioned that Mr and Mrs Arnold had decided to leave, though whether this was a decision of José Oswaldo's is not clear, and he does not appear again in the letters.

Orton, Bolivia

8 May 1899

My dear Nellie,

I hope that Dad's and Mama's coughs are better. I am afraid I shall be very miserable when I come back to the cold weather again. I am looking forward to a letter from Mama, she always writes me long ones, and when are some more photos coming?

I am going to a funeral this afternoon. For 3 days I have been trying to bring up a baby goat. Its mother died 2 days after it was born, so I took the poor little thing, it wanted to be cuddled the whole time; so we took it to bed with us and this morning it died, I am sorry to say, and I am going to bury it in the river.

We are going to move into another house this afternoon; this one with the zinc roof is too hot and makes my head ache. The one we are going to has a palm leaf roof and tile flooring. It has been nicely fitted up for us.

We have a lot of gentlemen staying here just now, so we have been very gay, dancing and playing games and riding horseback.

I don't think I have written since my birthday. We gave a little dance and enjoyed ourselves for 2 days. I had a lot of flowers from the forest given me, a nice scent bottle from Fred, and stuff for a dress from Mrs Arnold, also a silk shawl from my ironing woman.

We put up the English flag and fired off shots, and at 2 o'clock in the morning 3 gents serenaded me with guitars and Spanish songs.

I also had a nice cake with a tiny English flag stuck in it, which the cook gave me, and a piece of Maltese lace from his wife, so I did not come off badly; but there was no champagne or wine to be had in the whole river, so an old Negress here made me 8 bottles of a drink made from Brazil nuts; it looks like milk when it is finished but it is very intoxicating.

We have all been suffering from dysentry, but we are now better. We think it was on account of the water, the river being very high; all the dead trees, etc. come floating down and when there is no rain we have to drink river water.

Half of our time has now passed, thank heaven. I am longing to come back to Europe, but you must order specially fine weather for me, or make me a woollen sack to sit in.

We are expecting a photographer here soon, when we hope to send you all sorts of photos.

Now, goodbye dear Nellie, give my love to Dad, Mum and everyone, also from Fred too.

Your loving sister,

Lizzie

Tell Jack I wrote to him by this mail and hope he will receive the letter.

Dear Nellie,

I send my love to you and all. I hope you are all well; we are King and Queen out here, but people never know when they are well off. I am sorry, though, you could not come and stay with us.

Yours affectionately,

Fred

Orton, Bolivia
7 June 1899

My Dear Mama,

I received your letter dated Jan. 15th, also a parcel of books, for which I thank you very much. I like that new fashion book and was very glad of the pattern of dressing jacket. Since I wrote you last we have changed our abode and are now nice and comfortable. We bought a few rugs and odds and ends and our sitting room looks quite European; then we have a bedroom with 2 beds and a dressing room, also a corridor for the muddles and servants. I have had an Indian boy given to me of about 8 years and he beats any one of the English servants as regards work; he can do anything and he is so affectionate. He cried at first, but now he seems fond of me and Fred. We treat him as a sort of child and servant at the same time. I have also a nice Indian woman who looks after me well, as a sort of maid. She won't let me eat anything at all soiled and is so particular, she keeps the boy in order too; in fact we are now nice and comfy and feel at home.

Of course we had to give a house warming, and there happened to be a lot of passengers, so we were very jolly, dancing and singing until 3 o'clock in the morning, with an accordian and a guitar for the band.

We keep very well with the exception of small ailments, but 5 days down river there has been an epidemic of yellow fever and the people have been dying by the dozen, amongst them a good many friends of ours and my old man servant. A lot of sick people came up here to escape, and we have a house arranged for the Indians as a hospital. We have had 5 deaths only.

Yellow fever or Yellow Jack, as it was often named, had an evil reputation. The disease is endemic in certain parts of South America, and the Madeira remains one of the worst places. Without care, yellow fever is often fatal and during his campaign against Hispaniola (Haiti) Napoleon's general Rochambeau lost 23,000 of a force of 30,000 men. The fever, caused by a virus, develops within two to six days of the victim being bitten by the carrier, the Aëdes mosquito. It is a difficult disease to eradicate as the virus is maintained in forest animals, especially monkeys. Epidemics can begin when a person who has become infected in a yellow fever area travels with the disease to a fever-free place where, if there are Aëdes mosquitoes in the vicinity, the disease transmission cycle is started again. Lizzie, though, was hopeful.

The weather has now changed very cold, so the fever will now pass away. Orton is very healthy but down where the fever is, is the first waterfall, and in low water time is very unhealthy.

It was then June. The river level was falling quickly and the *surs* were beginning.

I received a letter from Bib, also one from Alice. I hope Bib is better. Anaemia is one of the chief complaints amongst the Indians here, I think it is on account of their food. We are getting short of cattle and can only kill twice a week instead of 3 times, so they live mostly on dried meat and rice and bananas. For 2 days it has been so cold, I have to go about with a shawl and my bath of rain water was like ice.

I am glad Dad is better and I hope he will feel strong enough to take his trip to Switzerland.

Orton, Bolivia
19 August 1899

My dear Mama,

A few days ago I received a nice budget of letters from you dated March 27th, also from Jack, Bert, Bib and Rosie and Mrs Limberger, so I was happy. I also received the books and music for which I thank you very much.

Before answering your letters I will tell you what little news I have. Fred was away for a month in the fever parts, but came back quite healthy, thank heaven. I was in a fright the whole time. He did not return in time for our fete the 6th August as there was a slight accident to the launch. During this voyage he managed to save the life of a boy who fell overboard during the night and would have been drowned but for Fred. They made quite a hero of him on the launch.

We had a great feast here for 2 days, the 6th and 7th August, the national day of Bolivia. Our one street, as we call it, was decorated with flags and Chinese lanterns. The first performance was at 6 o'clock in the morning when they saluted the flag with shots and sang the national anthem. At 1 o'clock we all dressed awful swells (there were 4 ladies from the next village) and went to the corridor of the big house where seats were arranged. There they sang again the anthem and afterwards made speeches. At 2 o'clock there were shooting matches, horse riding, racing, sack races and all sorts of things got up by the Clerks. We made little bouquets of ribbon and flowers for the winners, which I presented, of course. They gave them to the ladies and I came out with the largest number. At 8 o'clock there was a grand ball which lasted until 4 o'clock. I had 2 lovely dresses which a visitor here made me; they looked as if they had come from Paris. I will enclose a piece of the one I wore in the afternoon; it was trimmed with lace and pale blue ribbon. The one for the ball was pale blue silk trimmed with some net veils which I had by me and pale pink ribbon. It was a dream and suited me splendidly; I was the biggest swell.

. . . On the 7th August the day was very much the same, only we slept all the morning. In the evening we danced until 2 o'clock. On the 8th August Fred arrived, so we gave a ball in our rooms. It was the nicest of the 3 dances and lasted until 3 o'clock. The band consisted of an accordian, a flute, guitar and a zither which a lady brought with her. We all enjoyed ourselves immensely, though we missed Fred very much, he is the only good dancer here. So you see, we are not quite out in the backwoods.

I must say that since we have been here the people are more civilised, they dress better and are more polite. Fred keeps them up to it.

The mosquitos are terrible, I had quite 3 dozen in a piece of paper which I murdered whilst writing this letter, but my black-bird has carried them off, otherwise I would have sent them to you. They are splendid in the soup, we eat a lot of them in the season.

About a week ago a lady arrived from one of the villages in the Madre de Dios where we stopped for some time. She said that the Indians, who are half savages, have killed her husband and 2 servants. She managed to save herself and 2 children and a gent by pushing out a canoe in the middle of the river. They then travelled until they arrived at the next village. After some days a party set out to see how matters were; they found the house and everything destroyed and the Indians gone off to the forest. One is never safe with the half civilised Indians and we don't know how we passed through all those savage parts to safety.

The poor woman has absolutely nothing except the clothes she had on when she escaped, though the people are kind and gave her many things. I don't think I should have the courage to do our journey over again, knowing the people as I do now. We shall come home by the safest route, goodness knows when; how I am longing for the next 2 years to pass.

The 'Anta' of which Lizzie speaks in her next letter was a tapir – when young they are pale, dullish brown, with almost white broken stripes. Older animals have extremely short grey-brown hair and are the heavyweights of the South American mammals – some adults weigh as much as 400 lb. Tapirs have a short, flexible snout which they use for browsing and, although they spend much of their time in the forest, they will readily take to the river.

Dirt- and clothes-eating is a sign of severe malnutrition. The instrument with which the Indians were beaten was a short stick armed with four knotted rawhide lashes.

Orton, Bolivia
10 October 1899

My dear Mama,

I am glad you are all in pretty good health. We are well, but I am afraid we shall not be able to stand more than our 5 years, it is a very trying position. We are now King and Queen of Orton (Mr and Mrs Arnold having left for Europe). We have 500 Indians at our disposal and about 500 Bolivians, clerks, etc. It is no joke I can assure you to keep them all in order and happy at the same time; they are like children and one has to listen to their little troubles, etc. I was afraid at first when I had to take command, but they all seem to like us very much. Fred has a tremendous lot to do, he has to work until 10 o'clock at night.

My family has increased. The latest is an Anta, I don't know whether you have seen one in the Zoo. He is like a small elephant. He sleeps from 9 in the morning until 7 at night, then he has a good feed and goes off to the forest for the whole night; then he has a good swim in the river and comes back to me, to smack him, etc. which he enjoys immensely. Then he goes to sleep for the day.

Interval of half an hour.

Just at this minute 3 children came along to ask me to go to the forest with them to look for flowers. We went and got caught in a storm. I told them to run but I couldn't so I got wet through, had to change everything. I wish you could see the flowers we bring back, tremendous red passion flowers, white lillies, all sorts of curious and different coloured flowers. But they only last one day in water, so nearly every day I go with half a dozen children with their knives behind me; I always have my table nicely decorated.

I am glad Dad is better. I wish I could send him a little of the summer here, but I am afraid he would say a big D—— to the mosquitos and flies, which always accompany the hot weather.

That poor little savage girl I wrote to you about, died the other day; she would eat her clothes, also dirt, until she was almost a skeleton. In one night she would eat nearly half her chemise and it is impossible to cure them. It is true that you at home cannot realise the true state of things here. It wants a tremendous lot of patience to civilise the people here; they always have a longing for their old life, they run away for 3 months, 6 months and very often longer. We send after them, and then give them 100 lashes; it is the only remedy, of nothing else are they afraid. If you are kind they take advantage and steal everything possible. I have been very fortunate, the only thing my woman steals is to eat; they have tremendous appetites.

You need not feel nervous about our life here, we have the best of everything here; we command, nothing else; at a moment's notice I can have a dozen strong Indians to do whatever I want them to, and they like to work for me because I always give them a drink.

From your loving daughter,
Lizzie

[Orton],
16 November 1899

Dear Mama,

Think this will arrive about New Year's Day. We both send you our best wishes for the New Year and hope you will have spent a good Xmas.

I hope Jack received my letter in time for the Xmas stockings. It is some time now since I received news from you, the last was dated June 5th and you were all thinking of summer holidays; how I would like a fortnight at a bracing seaside place, to be able to breathe and eat something nice. The mosquitos are simply fearful, I have killed at least 30 whilst writing.

We are both well but a tiny bit worn out with entertaining visitors. As soon as one batch goes off another arrives, and to look after the table and make conversation with people whom you have never seen is rather a strain. This morning we are for once alone, but this afternoon will arrive a launch with goodness knows who.

Tell Louie my waist is not a scrap bigger. I can still wear the stays which I wore when I left London, but only on state occasions as they are too hot. I am afraid if I send her my left off dresses she will have to get Bert to make her a patent foot warmer lining. My bicycle she can have with pleasure if she will fetch it, but I don't know where it is.

Is Bib getting better? What does she take for medicine?

I don't think I have any more news for you. We hope that you will all keep well. We have only 2 more years to wait now; you don't know how I am longing to come home and Fred too . . . .

Now goodbye dear Mum, we both send our love to you all.

Your loving daughter,

Lizzie

Fred delayed writing the next letter home until a *lancha* was heading downstream to the Madeira.

> The Orton (Bolivia) Rubber Co. Ltd, Orton
>
> 9 January 1900

Dear Father and Mother,

I don't know how to tell you, but it is only too true. Our poor Lizzie died on the 18th of last month at half past nine in the morning. She was quite well until two days before, when she took to bed with fever and 'ere we knew where we were and what to make of her illness, her heart was attacked and she passed quietly away. She died happy and brave, like the good girl she always was, and if there is a heaven she has gone there, that we all know. The whole river is mourning her, for she was not only the little queen, but the angel of the place, good and kind to the poor, faithful and true to her husband.

Of my own grief and I need not speak. I was, and still am, half mad.

We buried her in our garden and the inscription on her cross reads:

> Lizzie Hessel
>
> died in Orton 18th Dec 1899
>
> Beloved by all

There is also an epitaph in Spanish by the people of the place, of which I will bring you a photograph. For the present I have had a wooden rail put round the grave, until the iron one which I have ordered is ready.

I do not, however, mean to leave her. When the time comes I will take her remains to England with me. Meanwhile I shall probably take a trip home in March to see you and cry once more over the sad fate of our beloved girl.

A Mr W. Drapper is going home shortly. He was present when she died and will look you up.

And now, in this heavy time of trial, I would like to say one word more. You know that my people are all doing fairly well, and if you, with your large family, should at any time be glad of the help of a son, will you consider me as one of them? I ask it as a favour. Let no false pride stand in the way, for the sacred memory of our beloved Lizzie.

With love to all and hoping that you will bear up with me in this hour of grief and sorrow. I am,

Your sad and faithful son,

Fred

Chapter Ten

'How inscrutable are the ways of destiny'

Two days later, on 20 December 1899, the *Gaceta* carried a full-column obituary headlined 'Sra. Isabel de Hessel'. 'The icy hand of death has cut off in its prime a precious life . . . all who had the good fortune to know her will never forget her friendly sweet nature. How inscrutable are the ways of destiny.'

When he next wrote home Fred gave a further short account of Lizzie's death.

> It was so sudden that I could not even send for more medical assistance. When the boat was leaving the harbour to go to Riberalta in search of it, the fatal hour struck. Still our doctor here did all he could to save her, and we must try to find consolation in the thought that it was God's desire to take her away and that His will must be accepted, though it does seem cruel and unjust.

In his letter to John and Sarah Mathys dated 9 January Fred mentioned a fever, and it appears that it developed quickly – perhaps an indication that Lizzie had caught yellow fever, though in this part of the Amazon she might have fallen victim to one of several common tropical diseases. Yellow fever, however, is an acute disease with a sudden onset; the symptoms are headache, chill and pains in the back and limbs. Anyone newly arrived from healthier parts can be affected seriously. And while Lizzie said the area was healthy she had also described the poor food and unhygienic conditions of the journey, which may have been a contributory factor.

In early 1900, business life at the Orton *barraca* turned again to the ongoing problems of ownership. José Oswaldo left for Europe only two days before Lizzie died, and his departure was announced in the *Gaceta* on 3 January. Fred, too, planned to leave. He asked his friend Kanthack in Pará to send a telegram to his cousin Joseph Limberger: 'Lizzie Hessel died 18th December, Fred returning soon.' Limberger wrote immediately to Ben Edwards and asked him to break the news gently to the Mathys family, since Fred's letter could take six months to reach them. Even so, the sad message took two months to reach 83 De Beauvoir Road, and throughout this time Fred was suffering from grief and the strain of the serious problems facing the *barraca*. The *Gaceta* noted that 'the worthy manager is in poor health' and surmised that his condition was due 'to his misery'. He had told Jack in a letter:

A short while before she expired, poor Liz made me sit by the side of her bed and her last words to me were: 'We are both very affectionate, aren't we? Fred, I have been cross with you some-times, and yet you have always been so kind to me.' She passed away smiling on all, like the angel she was.

On 25 April, the *Gaceta* printed a 'Notice' signed by Fred to pass the authority at Orton into the hands of a Señor José Fechter – Fred must have definitely decided to go. The Acre situation was not good and that too may have influenced his decision. Galvéz and his cronies were bickering among themselves, so the Bolivian government took the opportunity of sending a small contingent of soldiers from the city of Cochabamba, some 500 miles away, to force the surrender of the revolutionaries and establish a Bolivian 'presence'.

The Bolivian troops defeated the separatists in two skirmishes – one at Puerto Alonso and the other in the even more decrepit backwater of Rio Sinho. To add a convincing deterrent against further interference, the Bolivians threw a number of corpses into the Acre River to float downstream as a warning to the Brazilians. According to Fred's nephew, still alive today in the United States, his uncle had fought with the rank of colonel in some Bolivian revolution, so it is possible that he was involved here. At about this time Fred left Orton and set out on the long journey across the Andes to La Paz, the Bolivian capital.

As the crow flies it is not much more than 400 miles, but the only route that Fred could take was along the tributaries of the Beni River upstream through rapids into the mountains. Even now the land route is not to be taken lightly, as the lower forested Andes are a tangled wilderness notorious for their many venomous snakes and local endemic diseases. The mule paths followed by Fred are still used by Indians and local farmers; the tracks zigzag upwards, following the maze of valleys and ridges below the snowcaps. Often the trail descends to cross a tumbling river before continuing the climb, thus adding thousands of extra feet. In some places the paths have been blasted from sheer rock faces, making a ledge so narrow that it is impossible for uphill and downhill traffic to pass. Dizzying canyons 2000 or 3000 feet deep have to be crossed on logs wedged into cracks on the rock face, and once the humid forest is left behind at about 9000 feet ice, hail and snow blast the trail. It was in one of these places that Fred's mule slipped, as his nephew remembers: '. . . carrying all Lizzie's belongings it fell 3000 feet'. The diary which Lizzie had written so assiduously in such extraordinary conditions was lost, but Fred survived and completed the journey.

From La Paz he probably crossed Lake Titicaca on one of its British-built steamers. At 12,500 feet, Titicaca is the world's highest navigable lake, and the twelve-hour steamer crossing covers 120 miles, finishing at the small lakeside town of Puno. This was the route used in 1877 by James Orton, who died while crossing the lake and is buried on the Isla de Estevas, an island near the entrance to Puno harbour and now the site of a luxury hotel.

From Puno Fred's quickest way to Europe was by train down the Andes to the Pacific port of Mollendo, then by steamer south to the Strait of Magellan in the icy southern extremity of the continent. The sea route leads into the Atlantic, and at the turn of the century British ships often called at the Falkland Islands before heading for home.

By 1902 Fred was back in England, living in Croydon Road, Beckenham, Kent; along with other creditors, including Pedro Suárez and Baron Jacques de Gunzburg, he now tried to get his money back from the Orton (Bolivia) Rubber Co Ltd., which was in voluntary liquidation. Fred's petition was opposed, and among the company papers in London there is no evidence to suggest that Fred had ever seen the 'company' transferred to him in Riberalta in April 1899.

The events of the next decade are among the blackest in the history of the Amazon. Lizzie's adventure was cut off as the rubber boom was gathering momentum, yet within her letters there is evidence which, if it had been known at the time, could have changed the lives of thousands.

The power struggle along the Brazilian frontier, handled brashly by Galvéz and unsubtly by the politicians, was rekindled in July 1900 at about the time when the bodies of the revolutionaries were floating quietly downriver and out of Bolivian territory. After gaining control, the Bolivian government looked for a way to finance the development of the territory and offered an enormous land concession on the London and New York markets. The deal covered approximately 75,000 square miles of the Acre within a particular interpretation of the boundary of Bolivia and extending to the little-known upper reaches of the River Javari. The concession allowed the right for five years to purchase land at a nominal rate of four centavos an acre, with navigation and mineral rights included. The annual net profit could be tax-free for sixty years, though Bolivia was to receive 10 per cent from three years after signing. The concessionaires were to be rent collectors and could take up to 40 per cent of the dues in the region; they were also to maintain law and order. This Acre Concession amounted to a state within a state, and the business was agreed with an Anglo-American company, the Bolivian Syndicate of New York, registered in London and New York. Among the syndicate were members of the Vanderbilt family and a cousin of Theodore Roosevelt, then President of the United States. A British member of the syndicate, Sir Martin Conway, was granted a smaller 15,000-square-mile concession with a fifty-year tax exemption on the edge of the Andes.

The effect of such a massively capitalised foreign involvement in the heart of the Amazon was felt immediately. Brazil closed the Amazon to Acre traffic and did not recognise the concession. A group of Brazilians in the Acre claimed independence from both the syndicate and Bolivia; so with options dwindling fast, both countries despatched troops to the Acre. An unknown correspondent, possibly one of the syndicate, complained:

It is hardly to be tolerated by the great capitalist countries such as the United Kingdom and the United States, that the legitimate efforts of their sons to open up the trade and resources of a comparatively small country, not indeed populous, should be thwarted by the mere jealousy and short-sighted selfishness of Brazil.

So, with acrimony boiling and battle lines drawn, Bolivia and Brazil seemed set for a clash.

On the morning of 26 January 1903, the fifty-two-year-old Bolivian President, General Don José Manuel Pando, led the 5th Infantry Battalion out of the city of La Paz. Its destination was Acre, three months' journey away, and the intention was to relieve the small garrison of 250 men of the 3rd Infantry Battalion commanded at Puerto Alonso by Coronel Canseco. Crowds thronged the squares and steep thoroughfare where, according to one eyewitness, everyone joined the marching soldiers. Women and men with flags and handkerchiefs cried and cheered as the troops headed for the mountain passes.

General Pando had to descend the same tortuous route that Fred had used for his exit from the Beni. But tiny Bolivia did not stand a chance, even though along the Amazon frontier Nicholás Suárez was already defending his country's honour. Suárez had drawn together and trained 250 rubber tappers, whom he had armed with Winchesters. Don Nicholás had no shortage of ammunition or money; he also had launches, so his Columna Porvenir, as the force was known, was stationed at a strategic point on the Tahuamanu River.

Among localised conflicts the Acre war gets little mention. Few records have survived, though one by Elias Sagárnaga of the 5th Battalion was published in 1909. The troops arrived in Riberalta on 12 March and were welcomed personally by Don Nicholás, local officials, representatives of the House of Braillard, bands and a crowd singing the Bolivian national anthem. The fighting was over – they had arrived too late. Suárez had held out for as long as he could – several weeks – before more forces and naval contingents arrived from Brazil to support the Acreano rebels. The Acre was quickly annexed. Even so, General Pando's force moved on down the Beni River in launches including the *Sernamby*, the *Esperanza* and the *Tahuamanu*, which had been launched before Lizzie died.

Sagárnaga described Nicholás Suárez as being in charge of the liquidation of the Orton Company and the disposal of Vaca Diez' house, which was the 'grandest that existed in the Beni'. On the afternoon of 27 March they arrived at Orton itself, 'a relic of the magnificent, fantastic conceptions of Señor Vaca Diez'. The troops stayed overnight in the 'lavish rooms' before moving on the next day to the Orton River and the Acre. They made a strong show of the Bolivian presence along the still undetermined border. That month Bolivia agreed that Brazilian troops should occupy the Acre River, though Bolivia was to hold the Orton and Abuna.

Aghast at the swift change of ownership, the Bolivian Syndicate prepared to sue for damages and eventually came out of the affair with £110,000. By the Treaty of Petropolis in 1903 Bolivia lost a slice of land approximately the size of Great Britain and received in return 2000 square miles close to the Madeira River and £2,000,000 indemnity from Brazil, mostly to be used in the building of railways. At last the Madeira–Mamoré railway dream was revived; Bolivia and Brazil were to have equal rights along the track, and its construction was to be Brazil's responsibility.

In gratitude for services rendered, the Bolivian government gave Don Nicholás a concession of almost 8000 square miles in the Beni. But even Suárez couldn't manage that amount and he continued to consolidate, taking over Orton in the process.

In 1904 John Mathys died in Hackney aged seventy-six after a long illness, and the family gathered to mourn. In the same year Gregorio Suárez was killed by Caripuna Indians at the Madeira Falls. It is family history that Gregorio recognised some of the Indians along the river, so when they offered a friendly greeting he went ashore. During a simple challenge match to test their shooting skills – the Indians were fascinated by revolvers – the show somehow turned sour. An arrow went through Gregorio's heart as a signal for the Indians to set about slaughtering his companions. By hiding beneath an upturned canoe two of Gregorio's men escaped and subsequently made their way upstream to tell Nicholás of the disaster. Suárez immediately filled a boat with men and guns and moved smartly downriver to the scene of the ambush, but the Caripunas had fled. Nicholás trailed them deep into the forest where he found the Indians drinking cognac and ripping open boxes of stores that Gregorio had been ferrying. Gregorio's head was stuck on a spear in the middle of the clearing. In revenge, Nicholás surrounded the camp and killed every single Indian. The message soon went out that Suárez was not to be fooled with and the portages along the Madeira would be kept open.

Lizzie's own story was lost in the welter of events as the rubber boom soared. Many of the rubber men she had met made news as scandals sent waves across the Amazon. By 1906 the price of rubber was rising sharply towards the three dollars per pound mark, and dizzy fortunes were being made. The Peruvian Julio César Arana, whom Lizzie would have heard of when she was staying with Mr Weiss at Iquitos, moved to Manaus and then London, where in 1907 he registered the Peruvian Amazon Rubber Co. Ltd, later floated on the stock market as the Peruvian Amazon Co. Ltd, with a capital of £1,000,000 and a registered office in the City. Among the directors was Henry Read of the London Bank of Mexico and South America, who had earlier provided Arana with credit. Two of the other six directors were British – John Russel Gubbins, who had long experience of Peru, and Sir John Lister-Kaye, whose background was impeccable. But despite these credentials two unrelated problems arose. First, the shares were a flop, and then in a scandal of historic proportion Arana's company prospectus was seen to be a fabrication. He claimed that his company had vast territorial rights to land bordering the Putumayo River where 'there lived 40,000 Indians who were being taught to improve on the crude methods already being used for processing rubber'.

In May of the previous year Percy Harrison Fawcett, a thirty-nine-year-old Royal Artillery major, set out for the Beni, Orton and Acre. Like Arana, Fawcett was determined and completely undaunted by Amazon conditions. But there the similarity stopped: Fawcett was an artist who had exhibited at the Royal Academy, he designed yachts, he dabbled in archaeology, and like his brother Douglas he was regarded as a philosopher. He was in the Amazon because the Bolivians, through their embassy in London, had requested the Royal Geographical Society to act as a referee for their numerous boundary settlements. Fawcett, who held a Royal Geographical Society Diploma in Surveying, was seconded to a special boundary commission destined to work for several years in the Amazon forests.

It is unlikely that Fawcett and Arana ever met, as their creeds and places of work were far apart. Arana's enterprise in the distant Putumayo was based on the rapid expenditure of trees. The region was rich in the *caucho*-producing *Castilloas*; once tapped, the trees died, and, perhaps coincidentally, Arana's belief in disposables extended to the 40,000 local Indians, mainly Huitotos. Arana's Putumayo was a 'closed river', where he employed a polyglot gang of agents and managers to extract as much work from the Indians as their bodies could stand. The agents used Barbadian overseers – well used to the heat; black, so they could be recognised; and, better still, British subjects. After all, it was a British company. . . . To round up fleeing Indians the agents employed an army of teenage boys – 'carabineers' – armed with Winchesters.

Few accounts of the brutal excesses of the rubber boom have been published. The best documented and the one which created a public outcry was the report from the Putumayo forests north of Iquitos. Another separate account originated from the diaries of Major Fawcett who was in Bolivia at the time. British involvement demanded a British enquiry and arguments as to who was responsible for the conditions were passed from office to office. And Lizzie's letters, unknown at the time, would have supported many of the claims made by Fawcett. As the authorities discovered, the Beni became as closed as the Putumayo.

Flogging was the accepted way of starting a day and dealing with Indians in the Putumayo. As Lizzie had written from Orton: '. . . and then give them 100 lashes, it is the only remedy, of nothing else are they afraid'. Perhaps after so many adventures where she had been close to death she felt that these outrageous Amazon interludes were like crossing the road. And to the locals the Indians were 'animals and not people'. But flogging was just the beginning, and behind the scenes the rubber boom produced an orgy of terror unlike anything seen in South America since the *conquistadores* arrived.

It could not last. Eventually the callousness and brutality of the Amazon rubber industry were exposed. *Truth* magazine in London led the way in their September and October 1909 issues with first-hand accounts of the Putumayo and the affairs of the Peruvian Amazon Co. Ltd. The story came from a twenty-three-year-old American railway engineer, Walter Ernest Hardenburg: 'They flog them inhumanely until their bones are laid bare . . . they do not give them any medical treatment but let them linger, eaten by maggots till they die, to serve them afterwards as food for the chief's dogs.' With another American, W. B. Perkins, Hardenburg had set out to follow the difficult route from the Colombian Andes downhill to the Putumayo. Their intention was to reach Manaus and find work on the Madeira–Mamoré railway.

Travelling by canoe along the easy-flowing, level Putumayo, Hardenburg and Perkins found a fresh nightmare at each bend in the river. First, they were unwelcome, since Arana's men had virtually taken over a large corner of Colombia. Next, the two Americans realised they had seen so many atrocities that their own lives were in danger. The *Truth* articles and Hardenburg's account in his book *The Putumayo: The Devil's Paradise* reveal the style of punishments meted out to labourers who failed to reach Arana's predetermined rubber quota; or for any other reason the agents could suggest. The Indians were terrified by the system and usually fled. Then, Hardenburg said,

> They take his tender children and torture them until they disclose the whereabouts of their unhappy father. Their favourite mode of torture is by suspending them from a tree and building a fire beneath them . . . another method of punishment is that of mutilations such as cutting off arms, legs, noses, ears, penises, hands, feet and even heads. Castrations are also popular punishment for such crimes as trying to escape or being lazy, or for being stupid, while frequently they employ these forms of mutilation merely to relieve the monotony of continual floggings and murders to provide a sort of recreation.

Long chapters of cruelty are packed into Hardenburg's indictment. Of Iquitos he said: 'Every steamer that goes to Iquitos loaded with rubber from the Putumayo carries from 5–15 little Indian boys and girls who are torn sobbing from their mothers' arms without the slightest compunction.' As Lizzie said in Orton, 'He cried at first, but now seems fond of me and Fred.'

The Putumayo Scandal turned out to be long and tortuous, involving the Foreign Office, Members of Parliament, statements in *The Sunday Times* and eventually Roger Casement, then British Consul-General in Rio de Janeiro and already well known for his investigation of atrocities in the Belgian Congo. The principal allegations in London, though, focused on British responsibility in the Amazon. How had a British company come to get involved with such a degrading business? And since at the time something approaching £600 million of British money was invested in South America, what other skeletons might this particular cupboard be concealing?

Casement went to the Putumayo in late 1910 with a commission of enquiry, and his preliminary report, delivered to the Foreign Office early the following year, confirmed Hardenburg's story. Casement gathered information and signed statements. One was from a Barbadian, Westerman Leavine, who had witnessed

an Indian chief who was burned alive in the presence of his wife and two children, the wife was then beheaded and the children dismembered . . . an Indian woman was cut to pieces because she refused to live with one of the employees and the woman was wrapped in the National flag soaked in kerosene, set alight and then shot.

The Casement report was first held back and then, under pressure of intense public interest, released. People in Britain and the United States wanted action and believed that heads should roll.

Fred must have known there was scandal under the surface and perhaps heard of reports in *El Comercio*, a leading and conscientious daily newspaper in Lima which had repeatedly drawn attention to the ill-treatment of Indians. Not only did the paper cite the Putumayo, but earlier had pointed to the use of slavery in the Madre de Dios and neighbouring rivers. In February 1906 *El Comercio* reported the barbarous custom of slave raids, organised by the 'authorities themselves or by the rubber merchants'.

At the time of the Putumayo Scandal many letters and reports passed between London, the United States and South America. The international row was fuelled by more revelations and the blame moved around the world faster than the paperwork. One British army officer, Thomas Whiffen, on half-pay following a Boer War injury, had been exploring beyond the Putumayo: 'It is very common to see an agent with twenty concubines, or even thirty, many of them children of but 10–12 years of age.' Comments appeared from people who 'knew' what was happening but had said nothing at the time. British registered companies with Amazon connections were scrutinised in case another 'Putumayo' had been pushed under the carpet.

Suárez' enterprises were an obvious parallel and the Foreign Office began to check on affairs in the Beni. The Minister in La Paz, Cecil Gosling, sent reports to the Foreign Secretary, Sir Edward Grey, in London. Reputable travellers were consulted and Major Fawcett reported that it was quite normal for labourers on Bolivian rubber estates to receive up to 600 lashes. In his book, published many years later, Fawcett described how the floggings were given: 'The victim was spreadeagled flat on the ground – a soldier on each side gave a lash per second and the lashes were passed to a queue of waiting men who carried on without a break in the tempo.'

This discussion of conditions in Bolivia occurred in 1912 after Suárez had formed a new company, Suárez Hermanos & Co. Ltd; with a capital of £750,000 it was registered in London in 1909. Assets included

> Three steamers, two small launches and other small craft on the River Amazon. Six steam launches on the River Beni. Three steam launches on the River Mamoré and a number of boats – several cattle ranches – freehold properties – 20,629 *estradas* of rubber trees including 3500 at 'Colonia Orton'.

So Suárez had gained, but at what cost? Even Casement thought Fawcett had exaggerated in declaring that in his opinion fifty lashes would constitute a sentence of death. Official reports had to be accurate. Was it 50, 100 or 600? But Fawcett had been on the spot, and on several occasions in 1906 and 1907 had called at Riberalta: he also admitted that barbarities on the Orton River were not so obvious. Possibly this was true, as the cost of labour was high. Slaves were expensive and not to be disposed of lightly, as Fawcett realised when he was in Riberalta. Forest Indians, for sale with about thirty white people from Santa Cruz, were being herded by overseers with whips. The whites were being exchanged for the value of their debts.

All this was taking place soon after Lizzie had sent letters home to her parents telling them about the social life she was enjoying in Orton. But then Lizzie's letters were intended for the family, and her lost diary could have been different. However even some of the comments made literally between the lines about pets and sailor suits could have been useful for the investigators from all the governments involved – both Bolivia and Peru condemned the practices of the rubber bosses, and Bolivia had passed legislation in 1896 to protect rubber workers.

Any yarn emanating from the Amazon needs a strong second glance, and news from the rubber forests was no exception. When the United States Minister in La Paz, Mr H. Knowles, was asked to send a report to the State Department he said, 'It is practically impossible to obtain any accurate and reliable information in La Paz as to the conditions that prevail in the Beni Rubber Districts.' A reliable man, Mr T. Clive Sheppard, told Knowles that men left Santa Cruz for the Beni, and Santa Cruz was being depopulated. Asked about specific cases of atrocity or murder, Sheppard said he had heard nothing from a source that he would consider reliable – because, he said, no one actually returned to Santa Cruz to tell the tale: 'The tracks to the Beni are like the tracks – human footprints – to a bear's den. They lead only one way.'

The story at the time was confused. Fawcett, though a competent surveyor and explorer, was ridiculed and it seems he became the star of a cinema cartoon called *Colonel Hesaliar*. In London Pedro Suárez had succeeded his uncle, Francisco, first as Military Attaché and then as Bolivian Consul-General. Pedro countered the questions against his uncle Nicholás' firm and declared the Beni estates open to anyone wishing to visit them. That was in 1912, and in the following year Minister Gosling was refused entry. He reported home: 'I am convinced that the peonage as it obtains in the Beni is undisguised slavery.'

All the same, no one really knew what was going on and hard facts were needed. That one eyewitness account was elusive; yet it was concealed within Lizzie's letters. Just here and there Lizzie mentioned the slavery, and in one place in her letters – admittedly a statistically small and insignificant number of words in her total – she said, in July 1898:

We had a nasty scene here last night, an Indian tried to kill his wife but did not succeed. Four men bound him and laid him on the road and gave him 100 lashes. He screamed terribly. He was then shut up to have another 100 the next day. But he got away in the night and has not been seen since. It was fearful, but it is the only punishment they can give here, they don't care for anything else.

Lizzie's letters came to light too late. Her simple statement followed by 'I'm longing for Bert to come out' has a ring of truth. Had it been seen at the time of the Putumayo Scandal the world's financial markets might have wondered about conditions there too, and not been quite so willing to continue trading in Orton rubber – though perhaps that is a vain hope, considering the manipulations of international investment. Anyway, all this was happening at a time when South America was still young – not that it is much comfort to the Indians and peons who died with the rubber boom. The most that can be said is that the boom collapsed quickly.

Fred was in Antwerp when that crisis became a reality; it had been simmering for several years and, though not seen as a cause for panic, its possibility must have been considered when plantation rubber from the Far East first began to flow to London. The demise of the rubber barons had been initiated when Henry Wickham sent rubber seeds to England, long before Fred and Lizzie were married. As plantation rubber from the East reached Europe in quantity the Amazon was producing strongly, with exports increasing each year. The result was a glut and inevitably the world price slumped. Between 1910 and 1915 the price fell by 80 per cent. Financial disaster flooded through the Amazon. Pará was hit by a wave of bankruptcies. 'It would be difficult to find, in the entire world, another place more afflicted with troubles than Pará,' one journal commented, but of course it was worse upriver. The economics of the local trading system collapsed disastrously. In the old days the chain of debts starting with the rubber tapper in the forest to his supplier or middleman, whichever, was to the advantage of the men making the real money – hard cash, not credit. Suddenly, with lower rubber prices, the tappers could not even pay in rubber for the food they needed to keep themselves alive; in turn the middlemen could not pay their suppliers, and favours of paramours and perfume were worthless – no man could afford them, even in Manaus. Overnight the great cities emptied. The rubber barons and their concubines left for Europe, where their profits were secure.

Fred died in Antwerp in 1915, having suffered many illnesses, mostly the result of his time in the tropics. He never succeeded in his claim against the Orton Company. Europe at this time was inflamed by war and Fawcett returned to the army to become a Lieutenant-Colonel; he was awarded the DSO and four times mentioned in despatches. After the Armistice he returned to exploration and eventually disappeared inexplicably in the forests of Brazil. He had been awarded the Founders' Medal of the Royal Geographical Society.

Roger Casement was knighted for his work on the Putumayo, but less than four years later, in 1916, was found guilty of treason for his involvement with the Easter Rising in Ireland. Despite attempts by influential Englishmen, including Sir Arthur Conan Doyle, to secure his reprieve on account of his work for humanity, he was hanged. But Casement's report had toppled Arana's empire, and reddened a few faces in London. The brutal agents on the Putumayo were sent for trial in Iquitos – they escaped, it is said, with inside help. In 1922 the President of Peru ceded the Arana territory to Colombia.

The rubber boom had run out of steam by the time the Madeira–Mamoré railway was completed in 1912. The line had been built at enormous cost in lives and was too late. One train a week was all that those slack times warranted.

Suárez survived. Don Nicholás was a master businessman and had braced himself for trouble. With his feet firmly in London and his astute head for grasping a situation, his empire flourished by diversification. In the Beni he produced rubber and brazil nuts and bred cattle. Suárez, who had become known as the 'Rockefeller of Rubber', was at one time offered £10 million for his business; he refused. He and his wife divided their time between Bolivia and Hampstead until 1925, when Nicholás was seventy-three and they retired to Cachuela Esperanza. By 1931 the Suárez firm was fifty years old and its outposts were models of business efficiency; there was even an office in Guernsey. Shareholders in the company included many of the family and some employees. Nicholás kept working until three days before his death in 1940, at the age of eighty-eight. His tomb lies in the centre of the town, surrounded by the derelict remnants of his endeavours – his railway, a locomotive, warehouses, and a rusting Studebaker and Packard, cars he had imported to drive only a few miles on jungle roads. After a decline in Bolivia the company was finally wound up in London in 1961; its assets were valued at a mere £1500.

Lizzie's family is scattered. Her mother's family (the Trebles) emigrated to New Zealand. The Mathys family are in touch, but drifting apart with each generation. In his retirement one of Bert's children, Sir Reginald Mathys, decided to document the family history and filled a number of boxes with memorabilia, including Lizzie's letters. Sadly, he died before he could fulfil his ambition.

Of Lizzie's adventures just the letters and a handful of mementoes have survived. The Orton *barraca* was dismantled by Suárez and taken to the last tile to Riberalta. The ground where the building stood is uneven, and nearby a few cultivated flowers mark overgrown graves; Lizzie's cannot be identified. One memorial to Lizzie is carved on the Mathys' family stone in Chingford Mount cemetery: 'In Loving Memory of Elizabeth Hessel.' But her true epitaph was written much earlier, in Orton, when the *Gaceta* said: 'Before her tomb, which, as humble as her character, lies hidden in the forest, we do respectful homage.'

Acknowledgements

Ann Brown and Anne Rose would like to thank the following people for their help in compiling this book: Norman Blay, Ed Brown, Clive Charlton, Jim Curtis, Molly Cuthbert, Peter Fussell, Charles Hessel, Frederick A. Hessel, Jean Hessel, Doris Hughes, Roger Lawson, Barbara Mathys, Nicholas Mathys, Pete Middleton, Valerie Parson, Elizabeth Pinkney, Howard Rose and Steve Whitham.
Our thanks are also due to the numerous friends who took care of our children when we were away researching.

Tony Morrison would like to thank: La Academia Nacional de Ciencias, La Paz; Nicholas Asheshov, Lima; Robin Burnett, OBE, Belém; Nilda Cacéres, MBE, Lima; Canning House, London; George Clarke, Manaus; Richard Coutts, La Paz; Brian Fawcett; Steve Harrison, Santa Cruz, Bolivia; Mark Howell; David Lorimer, Iquitos; Gonzalo Montes, La Paz; Allan Reditt; Dr Franz A. Ressel, Santa Cruz, Bolivia; Trevor Stephenson, Lima; Dr Ovidio Suárez Morales, La Paz; and Johannes von Trapp, Vermont. Of the many members of the Suárez family, I would like to thank for their help in earlier researches Chavez, Fernando, Ricardo and Nicomedes Suárez.

All photographs are from South American Pictures
Tony and Kimball Morrison, except for those of Lizzie,
her family and associates which are from Ann Brown/Jim Curtis or
Ann Brown's collection, and the photograph of the house in Orton
which is from the Colonel P. H. Fawcett Collection.

Bibliography

BEATON, CECIL: My *Bolivian Aunt*, Weidenfeld & Nicolson, London, 1971.
COLLIER, RICHARD: *The River that God Forgot*, Collins, London, 1968.
FAWCETT, P. H.: *Exploration Fawcett*, Hutchinson, London, 1953.
FIFER, J. VALERIE: *Bolivia: Land, Location and Politics Since 1825*, Cambridge University Press, 1972.
FURNEAUX, ROBIN: *The Amazon*, Hamish Hamilton, London, 1971.
HARDENBURG, W. E.: *The Putumayo: The Devil's Paradise*, T. Fisher Unwin, London, 1912.
HOWELL, MARK: *Journey Through a Forgotten Empire*, Geoffrey Bles, London, 1964.
MATTHIESSEN, PETER: *At Play in the Fields of the Lord*, Random House, New York, 1965.
MATTHIESSEN, PETER: *The Cloud Forest*, André Deutsch, London, 1962.
ORTON, JAMES: *The Andes and the Amazon*, Harper and Brothers, New York, 1876.
PEARSON, HENRY C.: *The Rubber Country of the Amazon*, The India Rubber World, 1911.
SCHREIDER, H. AND F.: *Exploring the Amazon*, National Geographic Society, Washington DC, 1970.
SOUZA, MÁRCIO: *The Emperor of the Amazon*, Avon Books, New York, 1977.
TOMLINSON, H. M.: *The Sea and the Jungle*, Duckworth, London, 1912.
WEINSTEIN, BARBARA: *The Amazon Rubber Boom 1850–1920*, Stanford University Press, 1983.
WOODROFFE, JOSEPH: *The Upper Reaches of the Amazon*, Methuen, London, 1914.

Many other references to letters, maps and official papers exist in archives in Britain, the United States of America and South America.

Index